"Christine delivers a clear explanation of b . . . . while showing . . . g
practical ways to heal the brain . . . and impro . . . . ruggling with
your behavior or the behaviors . . . others, this boo . . . . great resource for
your family, friends, and co-workers."

— DANIEL G. AMEN, M.D.
CEO and Founder of Amen Clinics
Author, *Your Brain Is Always Listening*

"Christine brings home the fact that domestic violence leads to a variety of problems.
One of which, especially when the victim is hit in the head, can lead to cumulative
concussion injuries that go unrecognized yet have consequences on victims' overall
cognitive abilities as well as family dynamics. The brain is sensitive to blunt traumas,
so learning how to avoid these mini-concussions is extremely important. I recommend
Christine's book because she addresses both the victim and the abuser, while giving
the brain its due credit."

— HARRY KERASIDIS, M.D.
Neurologist based in Maryland
Author, *Concussion-ology*

"I have never read a book about abuse written for both the abused and the abuser.
This reality creates a profound and impactful experience. Abuse comes in many shapes
and sizes, and Christine manages to identify many common, and not-so-common,
forms which disrupt a healthy outlook and opportunity in life. Recognizing abuse is
important, and Christine recommends processing the effects with a qualified therapist
or counselor, which is critical to healing the past and also offers practical tools for a
healthier future. I highly recommend this book to anyone affected by, aware of, or
going through abuse!"

— HEATHER M. BROWNE, PSY.D.
Psychotherapist and Founder, The Healing Heart
Author and Poet, *Directions of Folding*

"Christine's help was an eye opener for me. She helped me to identify dynamics in some
of my family relationships that were very unhealthy, and work on becoming stronger as
a person. Talking to her is the best thing you can do to start taking steps into healing."

— PAULA R.
Orlando, Florida

"Christine's work has been, and continues to be, a life line, helping me through a
difficult family situation. Christine's own personal experiences have helped me to work
through similar situations. Thank you."

— RACHEL REES
Swansea, Wales, UK

"Christine's insights gave me the courage to fight for my marriage. Her ability to bring
understanding to my situation affected my awarenesses and changed my thinking and
behavior. I felt empowered with this knowledge, and with God's grace, fearlessly moved
forward. This has changed the dynamic between us all for the better."

— JOANNE GROSSO
Grow With Christine MasterClass Attendee

"Christine is one of the most intuitive and compassionate women I know."

— ALLISON CARUANA
Author *Where Am I? 40 Day Devotional for Trauma Survivors*

"Christine not only provides clear guidance, but also hope, which is crucial when stuck in an abusive relationship. Christine provides a path that helps to break the cycle of abuse."

— CARINA M. LEESON, ESQ.
Family Law & Collaborative Attorney

"As an attorney practicing in criminal defense and healthcare license defense, my clients are frequently coping with trauma from abusive relationships of many types. I have referred numerous clients to Christine for counseling, and each of them has reached out to me to express their deep gratitude for the newfound sense of clarity and purpose they have as a result of Christine's counseling."

— JONATHAN ROSE, ESQ.
Criminal and Professional Trial Attorney

"Christine's courage to be vulnerable by sharing her life experiences allows the reader to be connected on an intimate and deeper level of understanding of the intricacies and nuances of abuse and trauma. In the darkness of secrets and shame, Christine provides the light to the path of understanding, healing, and growth while increasing overall hope of ending cycles of generational abuse."

— RENEE CHEROWITZ, L.M.H.C.
Winter Park, Florida

"Christine writes about all kinds of abuse, including how drugs and alcohol can impair the judgment of the victim and abuser. In my line of work, helping people overcome addictions, I see abuse virtually every day and the related consequences on relationships, work, and home life. Christine provides clear guidance, as well as hope, which is absolutely critical when stuck in an abusive relationship."

— JUSTIN DANIELS, FOUNDER
Defining Wellness Centers™ (addiction treatment)
Best-selling author, *No More Vodka In My Orange Juice*

"I was in a mentally and verbally abusive relationship for years. Christine literally saved my life! Her expertise and guidance were paramount in my healing process and gave me hope and courage to move forward with my life."

— ANGIE HELGESON, INSURANCE EXECUTIVE
Maitland, Florida

"Christine provides clear guidance, as well as hope. Most importantly, she reminds the audience that indirect abuse is just as destructive as direct abuse in its capacity to breed dysfunction in our lives. Vulnerability is indeed Christine's super power, as she revisits her personal traumas to illustrate that retracing the past is the necessary ingredient for healing one's future."

— ANDREA M. BROWNRIDGE, M.D., J.D., M.H.A.
Child, Adolescent, and Adult Psychiatrist

"Christine is a leading expert on psychological and emotional abuse. She provides clear direction for those who have experienced confusion and disorientation following toxic relationships."

— CRISTINA ALLY, L.M.H.C., R.P.T., N.C.C.
President, Mental Health Counselors of Central Florida

Identifying

ABUSE

Family Secrets

EXPOSED

That Breed Dysfunction

Identifying

ABUSE

Family Secrets

EXPOSED

That Breed Dysfunction

CHRISTINE HAMMOND, L.M.H.C., N.C.C.

Foreword by Kristen Willeumier, Ph.D., Neuroscientist and author of *Bioback Your Brain*

Grow With Christine LLC | Orlando, FL

Published by

Grow With Christine LLC, PO Box 1048, Orlando, FL 32802
(407) 740-6838 | growwithchristine@gmail.com

Publisher's Cataloging-in-Publication Data
Hammond, Christine.

Abuse exposed : identifying family secrets that breed dysfunction /
by Christine Hammond. – Orlando, FL : Grow With Christine LLC,
2021.

p. ; cm.

ISBN13: 978-0-9601063-0-1

1. Family violence. 2. Victims of family violence--Mental health.
3. Victims of family violence--Rehabilitation. 4. Family violence--
Prevention. 5. Behavior modification. I. Title.

HV6626.H36 2021
362.8292--dc23

Project coordination by Jenkins Group, Inc. | www.jenkinsgroupinc.com

Interior design by Brooke Camfield

Printed in the United States of America

25 24 23 22 21 • 5 4 3 2 1

DEDICATION

To my children: May this book help to free you from the past,
grow you in the present, and inspire your future.

To everyone who has felt like a shell of their true self.

SUBMISSION

Like wanton mannequins windowed,
We concrete the arena—
The omnibus of society.

Provided with enticing raiment,
Then stripped naked only
To be robed more pleasing to our vogue conscience.

Mannequins—emotionless, spiritless, defenseless;
Spurious to life,
Purposed to imitate.

Poem by Judy Johnson (my mother)
August, 1962

CONTENTS

PART ONE
Abuse Exegesis
Retracing the Past to Heal the Future

PART TWO
Abuse Exhumed
Identifying Family Secrets

PART THREE
Abuse Exiled
How to Heal from Abuse

FOREWORD

Dear Reader:

Abuse Exposed should be a required read for everyone, as abuse, cloaked in its many forms, is pervasive and ubiquitous. Whether glaringly overt or subtly covert, its presence may be felt in our closest, most intimate relationships, in our places of employment, or within the organizations we routinely frequent. The truth is, in order to be consciously aware of it, we must become wise and informed of its verbal and nonverbal cues and become empowered with strategies in the art of communication and self-love, as Christine so beautifully illustrates in this book.

Much like the samurai warrior trains diligently for combat, you must sharpen your "mental sword" in order to detect abuse in its earliest stages so as not to allow it to infiltrate your mind. One of your most valuable assets is to hone your power of discernment and to recognize when it is happening in order to make the conscious, empowered, loving choice to free yourself from this cycle and live in greater peace. Christine has extensive expertise in this field, and she serves as your thoughtful, compassionate therapist who will take you into a space where restoration of your mental, emotional, physical, and spiritual well-being is possible.

—KRISTEN WILLEUMIER, PH.D.
Neuroscientist
Author, *Biohack Your Brain:
How to Boost Cognitive Health, Performance & Power*

INTRODUCTION

"DUCK NOW!"

A voice yelled deep inside me, I believe from God. Instinctively, I fell to the ground after walking into the darkened apartment, which was fogged from the stench of alcohol from my husband's drinking.

CRASH!

My favorite, foot-and-a-half-tall, blue and white, Chinese-printed vase flew over me and crumbled to the floor after smashing on the wall behind me. Despite being under attack, I thought to myself, *That's my vase!* It had been a special wedding gift from one of my best friends.

"GET OUT!"

Next I heard Peter, my husband of three tumultuous years, screaming at me to leave. I didn't have to hear it twice. Among his affair, abandonment, drinking, and drug use, it was finally time for me to move on. Ironically, it wasn't even my choice. Sometimes, a victim doesn't want to give up, so they give in and become the scapegoat, a trampled doormat, until it's too late—with a vase or something else heading for their head. I should have seen, or acknowledged, the warning signs. But when we were coming out of college, our hearts were bigger than our minds. At least mine was.

Since then, I've learned a lot about abuse. I've helped a lot of victims, abusers, and others caught in the inevitable train wreck. Now, my career puts me square in the middle of abuse and traumas of all kinds.

Abuse is like a virus that spreads in overt, covert, and even unintentional ways, breeding dysfunction within families, relationships, and the next generation of society. Obvious abuse is easy to identify, but many times abuse can be spread without the victim or abuser realizing it. Regardless, the abuse impacts our lives, our health, our wealth, and all that matters most to us. That's why I'm writing to you, on a personal level, so that we can retrace our steps in life and see where, when, and how we've been abused. Then, we will rewrite our story with a new perspective allowing us to grow from our past, and we will move on with the ability to identify and diffuse abuse in the future. I believe the concepts in your hands can transform an individual, a family, a community, a country, and the world. How? By identifying abuse throughout your life, learning how to rewrite your story, and being able to vaccinate against the virus forever. It starts with you and me.

Abuse can occur to people of all ages, in all levels of severity, and it has compounded effects throughout life. Whether the abuse came to you as a child, adult, or senior, or whether it was unintended or intentionally caused harm, destruction, or even murder, I believe it's time to:

- *Stop ignoring* the dysfunction in your life and family, and *be real* with the facts.
- *Stop lying* to yourself, and *be honest* with yourself.
- *Stop blaming others*, and *start exercising self-responsibility*.
- *Stop the hurting*, and *start the healing*.
- *Stop giving up*, and *find hope* with a new perspective.

Everyone has flaws. Everyone has been hurt. Everyone needs hope. Yet, too often abuse, whether overt or covert, breeds dysfunction from within the family unit, which passes on to the next generation. We may be one-of-a-kind as individuals, including how we were raised and our current circumstances. But, I assure you, we have a lot in common: The desire for love and happiness, feelings of hurt and sadness, and even abuse, which is that pervasive. It happens even when you don't know it.

These statistics begin to tell the story:

- 80% of abused children are abused by their parents.

- 90% of child sexual abuse victims know the perpetrator in some way, and 68% are abused by a family member.[1]
- In the United States, an estimated 1,770 children die due to abuse or neglect each year, and 75% of children who die due to child abuse or neglect are younger than three years old.[2]
- One in three teens experiences dating violence, according to Loveisrespect, a project of the National Domestic Violence Hotline.
- The CDC reports that over one in three women and about one in five men in the United States will experience intimate partner violence in their lifetime.
- More than one-third of the homeless population consists of families with children, according to the U.S. Department of Housing and Urban Development.
- At least one in ten Americans over the age of sixty has been abused, including physical, psychological, verbal and sexual abuse as well as financial exploitation and neglect.[3] Unfortunately, The New York State Elder Abuse Prevalence Study estimated that for every elder abuse known, there were twenty-four that went unreported.[4]

Look around you. For every four people you see, it is likely that one of them has been abused.

Abuse is inevitable throughout our lifespan. We can't avoid it, and the risk of becoming infected continues whether we like it or not. Broadly speaking, abuse can be experienced in two ways: directly or

---

1. U.S. Department of Justice. "Sexual Assault of Young Children," as reported in *Law Enforcement: Victim, Incident, and Offender Characteristics*. Bureau of Justice Statistics. Accessed February 21, 2014, http://www.bjs.gov/content/pub/pdf/saycrle.pdf.

2. U.S. Children's Bureau, "Fatalities from Child Abuse," as reported in the 29th Edition of the *Child Maltreatment Report* based on data from the National Child Abuse and Neglect Data System, 2018.

3. Lachs, M., & Pillemer, K. (2015). Elder abuse. *New England Journal of Medicine, 373*, 1947–56. doi: 10.1056/NEJMra1404688.

4. Lifespan of Greater Rochester, Inc., Weill Cornell Medical Center of Cornell University, & New York City Department for the Aging. (2011). *Under the Radar: New York State Elder Abuse Prevalence Study* (PDF).

indirectly. **Direct abuse** is the form we are most familiar with, and typically the most scary, because victims are directly involved. If you've been raped, then you know the horrors of direct abuse. On the other hand, **indirect abuse** affects us when we observe abuse, which conditions our mind and behavior to believe this abuse is acceptable, tolerable, even normal. These are often the "family secrets." For example, if you were a child in the vicinity of domestic violence, then you may have experienced indirect abuse, which may have led to other conclusions about marriage, family, and life in general.

We will expose the abuse that has bred dysfunction in your life. My desire is that this process will help to relieve you of the burden you're carrying. I hope you will find commonalities from my story, but more importantly I hope you will discover the abuse in your life and recover to the point of true healing. This is NOT a book about revenge, but it IS about getting the facts, re-framing the abuse, being able to empathize, and having strength to stand up for yourself, even if you're at your weakest.

In this book, I've included two ways of identifying the abuse in your life. First, I've provided my story to help jog your memory about past events. Second, I've included lots of examples of the different types of abuse, so you can flip right to that section quickly.

Before getting ahead of myself, let me admit to you a few of my own family secrets.

I AM A VICTIM OF INDIRECT ABUSE.

One of the first memories from childhood was at the tender age of two. My mother, brother, and I lived with our biological dad, Hank, in a small, sparsely furnished but clean apartment. My brother, one year younger than me, and I were playing in the living room when my parents started yelling at each other. Hank hit my mom multiple times before she fell onto the sofa. She was in agony, sobbing and scared. Wanting to comfort her, I brought my stuffed animals to her. Following my lead, my little brother did the same. I remember experiencing intense anger toward Hank. I wanted him to go away. I wanted him to stop. I hated him for making my mother cry. Observing this physical violence, I started a process of being accustomed and conditioned to the behavior, a form of indirect abuse, which would impact my life forever.

I AM A VICTIM OF DIRECT ABUSE.

About one year later, as a mere toddler, I was able to share the same unfortunate physical abuse that my mother felt. One afternoon at the playground by our apartment, my mother, her best friend, and two kids were playing with my brother and me. It was a gorgeous day, and we were having fun. My mom and her friend were sitting on the swings, my brother and a little boy were in the sandbox, and I was on the see-saw with the friend's daughter. I heard my mom crying and looked over to see her upset. Before I could think, my instinct was to jump off the see-saw immediately. Unfortunately, I was at the top end. As I fell to the ground, I reached down, and my body followed. My arm landed squarely over a small pit, giving gravity and nature just enough gap for my body to snap my arm from the fall.

I didn't feel the pain immediately, but the look on my mom's face signaled that something was wrong when I lifted my arm in the air. My mom ran back to the apartment to call for help (no cell phones back then) while her friend held me and asked me why I had jumped. I told her, "I saw Mommy crying."

By the time Hank came with the car, I was no longer in tears. We got into the car, and this time I got to sit on my mom's lap in the front seat. Incredulously, Hank started yelling, cussing, and raging at my mom.

"You stupid bitch! What the fuck do you think you're doing, calling me in the middle of the day. How dare you interrupt me from work?"

My mom was bawling, "She's hurt. Look at her arm. It's broken."

"Who the hell cares? She'll be fine!" he yelled.

By this point, I knew this was escalating and where it often led. Sure enough, Hank threw a right jab at my mother's face. But this time, I put my head between his fist and her face, taking the full force of the blow.

I don't remember anything after that, until awaking at the hospital.

While in the emergency room, a doctor walked in wearing the standard long, white coat with a name badge. He spoke in a firm but gentle tone.

"Want to tell me what happened?" he asked while starting the examination.

I told him about falling off the see-saw.

"Yes, that makes sense," he said. "Now, what about this mark on your face?" he asked, referring to the left side where I'd been hit.

I was still dazed and confused from being knocked out. I looked at my mom.

"She hit her head from the fall," she chimed in.

But the doctor saw other warning signs. He looked at my mom intently and asked with compassion, "May I have a look at those bruises on your legs?"

"No," she said.

"How did you get them?" he continued his query.

"I fell down the stairs," my mom answered.

"No, you didn't," I said, without realizing the possible repercussions. My mom turned her head to me and gave me that look that says, "Shut up or else." So, I did. When the doctor asked me how she got the bruises, I did not respond.

The doctor took a step back and sighed. I remember him saying, "There is help for people who are being abused." But my mom continued to deny it. "I'm going to leave you alone to think about this for a few minutes," he said.

After he left, I was more confused than ever. I looked at my mom and said, "You told me not to lie, but you just made me lie."

"We don't discuss family business with strangers. What happens in the family, stays in the family." When the doctor came back, I lied and told the story my mom wanted me to say. Funny, my grandmother used to say the same thing! For my mother and grandmother, and now me, we never admit to feeling hurt or in pain, even in dire situations.

Unfortunately, keeping secrets and suppressing painful feelings were passed down in my family.

I HAVE ABUSED OTHERS.

While in kindergarten, I was playing on the school playground at recess one day. I had long hair, which was braided in pigtails. One of the boys came over to me, grabbed my hair, and tied the pigtails to the monkey bars. I was stuck. He, and many other kids, were getting a good chuckle out of it. But I was furious, and I screamed for help. The playground teacher untied me and said, "He (the boy) was just playing around." It was then that I realized I could be one of two kinds of people: Those who get abused or those who do the abusing. At that moment, I decided I was no longer going to be abused any longer. I could be the bully or keep being bullied.

It started off small. I wanted chocolate milk with my lunch, but we couldn't afford the extra ten cents. So, I started picking on another kid I could intimidate until he gave me his. From there, I would threaten to hurt kids who wouldn't give me the fun stuff in their lunch. One day, a boy challenged me to a fight on the playground. Having learned some moves from watching Hank, I won the fight. After that, I was fighting nearly everyone who wanted to, during recess. Eventually, I had a group of kids who wanted to join, and we formed a gang. We would spend recess bullying, fighting, and intimidating. This didn't stop until my family moved, and I changed schools when I was in the fourth grade.

I Am a Mental Health Therapist.

From these brief examples of direct and indirect abuse, I'm confident that you can relate to some part of these stories. After dedicating my career to counseling, I've invested more than twenty-five years learning about abuse and treating others. I've started writing to help more people find healing, and I have amassed nearly 500,000 followers in social media. My time, therefore, is at a premium, so I don't work with "easy" cases. Instead, I take on clients with personality disorders such as narcissistic, sociopathic, borderline, obsessive-compulsive, and paranoid. I've seen thousands of clients, and nearly everyone has a similar story of abuse, just with different players and locations. I specialize in helping families, because I believe that's where generational chains can be broken.

This is why we need to get real and to be honest so that we can heal. Unless we fully admit that we can be part of the problem of perpetuating abusive behavior, it will never stop. It doesn't matter if the abuse is ugly, obvious, seemingly small, covert, justified, habitual, or generational, or done in ignorance, anger, or desperation. Abuse is abuse, and it has to stop.

- We need to put an end to unhealthy "family secrets" and to thinking that "What happens in a family, stays in a family" is a healthy response.
- We need to end the cycle of abuse passed from one generation to another.
- We need to stop holding contempt for our mothers, fathers, and siblings and try to understand the reasons why they misbehaved.
- We need to empower the victim, not for revenge but for forgiveness, and to end the cycle of abuse in the family.
- We need to heal the abuser, and it can be done.

While writing this book, I, too, had a realization about my career: My desire to get between the abuser and the victim is exactly what I do in counseling. It's instinctive. Even as a three-year-old, I wanted to get between the abuser and the victim, and I paid the price with a punch to the face. But through my experiences, I became unafraid of confronting abusers in an attempt to wake them up to the damage they are doing to others. I am able to empathize with the abused and teach them to trust their instincts. Every time this process occurs, real positive change takes place. There is hope. I have thousands of examples.

You're not alone. We can grow from this. We can vaccinate the next generation with healing.

OR ELSE

Unfortunately, we all can imagine the ugly, dark side of this possibility. If we don't do something, those obvious, or even little, warning signs never automatically improve. They always get worse. We don't have to look far to see how unreported abuse affects generations, considering what we've seen in the worlds of entertainment and sports like football, gymnastics, and swimming, as well as within religions and even corporations. For many women, the #MeToo movement finally gave them a voice, a legal response that has resulted in the arrests of powerful men like Harvey Weinstein, Bill Cosby, and Jeffrey Epstein. But true healing from abuse may still need to occur with the individual.

Whether the impact is felt directly or indirectly, the price can ultimately be suicide.

Self-abuse and self-harm, including substance abuse, leave people with no hope, no will, and seemingly no options. Ironically, some will cut themselves, a form of direct abuse, to relieve pain. Suicide is among the ten leading causes of death in the U.S., with 1.4 million suicide attempts reported every year.

Some will join the military to escape the family dynamic at home. Too often, they return from service to the same problems, bringing with them post-traumatic stress disorder (PTSD) or a traumatic brain injury (TBI). While not all veterans' suicides are PTSD- or TBI-related, the combination of emotional or biological injury and returning to a seemingly hopeless history of family abuse leaves many of our veterans homeless and feeling hopeless. Sadly, suicide is the outcome for an average of twenty veterans *per day*.

Experts say that suicide could increase due to the COVID crisis. Alcohol sales have skyrocketed during the quarantine period, as has domestic abuse.[5] When you put alcohol, abuse, and trauma all in the same room for an extended period of time, what do you think will happen? Then, the will to live on can be decreased, which leads to

---

5. Julie Bosman, "Domestic Violence Calls Mount as Restrictions Linger: 'No One Can Leave,'" *New York Times,* May 15, 2020.

suicidal thinking and ideation. That's a depressing thought for anyone. But we can build a bridge over this thought, and lead to new growth opportunities.

It didn't work out that way for my best friend. She took her life when I thought she had recovered from her abuse. She left me behind, along with her fiancé, unborn child, and parents. Imagine the impact rippling through her family. Even though she passed twenty years ago, I still grieve her loss and my friendship with her. Suicide is like that. It stays with you and doesn't leave.

Racism and the psychological as well as physical abuse that we have witnessed cannot be ignored. Police brutality seen on video has sparked protests worldwide and has opened the door for a discussion about racial differences and how our society has abused these differences. Racism is abuse at an individual and community level. It is designed to minimize the value of its victims while elevating the abusers. It is physical, emotional, verbal, mental, and financial abuse all rolled into one. That issue deserves its own book, so in this book, we're going to focus on more personal forms of abuse.

You can even abuse yourself with your own thoughts. You may call yourself a loser or tell yourself that you're stupid or that you're never going to succeed or get anywhere.

You can also abuse yourself with your emotions, like shutting them down and saying they're invalid or not worth anything and that you shouldn't be able to express them, or by telling yourself, *I shouldn't be feeling this way. I'm not allowed to feel this.* That's all **verbal** self-abuse.

Avoiding the problem never works.

Not realizing the abuse is even a problem. If it is not acknowledged, just gets worse and worse, like an unattended virus. I have a whole chapter on warning signs to go deeper into this subject.

WHAT IS ABUSE?

The word "abuse" can be used as both a noun and a verb. As a noun, it is the improper use of something or the cruel or violent treatment of an animal or person. As a verb, it is to use (something) to bad effect or for a bad purpose, to misuse, or to treat (a person or an animal) with cruelty or violence, especially regularly or repeatedly.

The problem with these definitions is that they're just vague enough for a person not to even recognize that they are being abused. So often, abuse isn't even acknowledged, remembered, or understood. In other words, you and I were abused in many ways, beyond the obvious types of abuse.

That's why it's time for *Abuse Exposed*. If we can identify the abuse from our past, we can heal our futures. Let's get started.

❊ ❊ ❊

Please Note: With the exception of mine, the stories and names that follow are all based on composites of actual individuals and events. Any similarities to real people are purely coincidental.

PART ONE

Abuse Exegesis

Retracing the Past to Heal the Future

Chapter One

Rewriting My Story

The abuse we've experienced, caused, or been impacted by did not start with us. You may be in the middle of an abusive situation right now, and there are steps we can take to help, but the first fault is not yours or the abuser's. The abuse actually started with our ancestors.

Certainly, "human brain development is created through continuing complex interactions of genetic and environmental influences,"[6] as one study—with 113 citations—concludes. The DNA passed to our parents has been genetically coded with personality traits, as well as health-related and abusive traits, just like the color of our eyes or skin. Additionally, abuse can take place in pregnancy. For example, if the mother smokes, drinks, falls, or gets hit in the belly, the unborn baby will also experience these while preparing for delivery.

---

6. Giedd, Jay N., lenroot, Rhoshel K., "The changing impact of genes and environment on brain development during childhood and adolescence: Initial findings from a neuroimaging study of pediatric twins," *Development and Psychopathology*. Fall; 20(4): 1161–75 (2008).

Immediately, we begin conditioning the already-abused newborn with our environments, personalities, and families, among other ways.

Our lives were imprinted by the history of our ancestors, grandparents, and parents, bringing with them a completely different paradigm from how we were raised. See the logic here?

Science backs up this generational virus. Here are a few more examples:

- **Parents Pass Down Abuse to Their Children:** One study of 610 parents investigated the relationship between patterns of inter-parental (or partner) verbal and physical abuse and the impact it had on their children. Among the findings, children who witnessed or experienced verbal or physical abuse were more likely to experience similar patterns in their own relationships, including psychological, physical, or sexual abuse encounters. "Witnessing inter-parental or intimate partner violence has been found to be associated with adolescents' own relationship abuse...Findings indicate that parents' relationship quality and abusive behaviors may have a long lasting effect on their children as they enter mid and late adolescence."[7]

- **Young Girls Become Violent, Self-Destructive When Family Breaks Down:** A 2018 study of 140 girls, ages thirteen through seventeen, who either attempted suicide, were violent, or reported no destructive behavior. *The study found that the girls with suicidal and violent behaviors reported a greater number and intensity of conflict and tense relationships between the family members from different generations.* "Emotional distance and hidden projections (related to diseases) were the most significant predictors of suicidal behaviors in the studied adolescent girls. Alcohol abuse by significant family members, especially by male family

---

7. Liu, W., Mumford, E.A. & Taylor, B.G., "The Relationship Between Parents' Intimate Partner Victimization and Youths' Adolescent Relationship Abuse." *Journal of Youth and Adolescence* 47, 321–33 (2018),

members, and a lesser role of hidden projections, were the most significant predictors of violent behaviors."[8]

- **Abused Children Become Depressed, Addicted Adults:** A study using data from the National Epidemiologic Survey on Alcohol and Related Conditions III surveyed adults over the age of 55. The study concluded that children raised in "high adversity" environments, or by parents with a substance use disorder (SUD), or who were abused, are more likely to have major depression and significantly higher rates of SUDs.[9]

For the rest of the chapter, I'm going to reveal several abuse milestones in my life. This exercise is designed to jog your own memories and identify scenarios when you may have been abused. I share these stories not to brag, or even for you to compare with. Instead, I hope you will find it therapeutic in several ways:

- Relating to the abuse. You're not alone.
- Opening your eyes to hidden abuses.
- Identifying pivotal moments in your life that changed you.

In my story to follow, look for all the possible ways my life could have been impacted through previous generations. I'll point out the major milestones that I've needed to rewrite. Additionally, you may find common ground on some of these offenses. Jot them down. Keep a journal of these memories.

HARD-WIRE PROGRAMMING

My grandmother played a big role in my life, raising me for a number of years. So, a lot of my hard-wiring comes from her. She died at the age of 101, about five years ago as of this writing. Her Hungarian father died

---

8. Sitnik-Warchulska, K., Izydorczyk, B., "Family Patterns and Suicidal and Violent Behavior among Adolescent Girls—Genogram Analysis." *International Journal of Environmental Research and Public Health* (2018).

9. Youngmi Kim, Kyeongmo Kim, Karen G. Chartier, Traci L. Wike and Shelby E. McDonald, "Adverse Childhood Experience Patterns, Major Depressive Disorder, and Substance Use Disorder in Older Adults." *Aging & Mental Health*, Nov. 26, 2019.

of the Spanish flu after fighting in World War I. After losing her dad, my grandma stayed in Hungary with her mom and brother. Without her dad, her mom was not prepared to raise the kids on her own. Soon, both she and her brother were put into an orphanage. I've been told that she grew up very much like "Madeline" in the famous childhood story. With a temporary family at the orphanage and the absence of loving parents, my grandmother bounced around from one foster home to another, sometimes with, and sometimes without, her brother.

These circumstances caused my grandmother to develop *paranoia*, also a warning sign of other direct abuse. She would never admit to the extent of any abuse, but she was always worried about us being captured and stolen by somebody. She also hated locked doors. We were never allowed to be in a bathroom with the door closed for too long, because, for sure, she believed something bad was happening, even if we were just taking a shower.

PARANOIA—A mental illness characterized by heightened, compulsive fears that may include delusions of persecution, unwarranted jealousy, and other realistic or unrealistic scenarios that drive suspicious behavior. Can be a chronic personality disorder and an aspect of schizophrenia, in which the person loses touch with reality.

Traveling alone at age twelve, she boarded a ship bound for New York City from Hungary, on a one-way mission to find her mother. Meanwhile, her mom, an American at that point, was "living the life" and married to a very wealthy man. My grandmother's mom decided her lifestyle was more important than raising her daughter, so they sent my grandmother to be raised in a convent. There, she learned to speak English, and later she would become an American. Bi-lingual, she was hired by the United Nations, followed by the U.S. Embassy in Hungary.

Back in Hungary, my grandmother reconnected with her brother, who was an officer in the Hungarian army. She married her brother's best friend. Her husband, or my grandfather, is old-time traditional Hungarian. We're talking nobility, with umpteen generations living in the same house. He grew up on a vineyard, and the seal of our family is at the Matthias Church in Budapest.

During World War II, literally as bombs were going off in Hungary, my mother was born.

My grandfather was an officer in the Hungarian army, which, of course, means that he was fighting for the Germans. He was sent to the Russian front and was part of the 12% who survived, returning to Hungary with a bullet wound in his right side.

At that point, my grandmother was raising four kids, while my grandfather was on the run as a wanted man. My grandmother's brother was taken and sent to Siberia, while my grandfather went into hiding. On foot, he managed to make his way to Paris and, rather magically, caught up with my grandmother and their kids.

From Paris, they found a ship heading for New York City, becoming a part of the immigrant movement following the war. My grandfather could only find work that paid well below his status. So, they moved to Valparaiso, Indiana, where they raised the kids until the oldest went to college. They decided to settle down for the next thirty years in Wheaton, Maryland. That's where I'm from. But, as you can see, my family history is written with abandonment, paranoia, and wartime death as well as a rich heritage in Hungarian culture, which is much different from American life.

My mother, who was born into war and later raised with an absentee mother, living in a foreign land as an immigrant, was naturally eager to create a life here in the States. But like her mother, her first years of life were tumultuous with war, moving to a foreign land with a new language, and very poor living conditions. She did well in school and went to the University of Maryland to study English. That's where she met Hank. With his Italian roots, his family didn't like Hungarians and didn't want them to marry. But they did. Nine months later, I arrived.

You would be surprised what young children can retain during those early formative years. I loved the Hungarian education that exposed me to the arts, and I was taught to play piano and appreciate theater. Between the lines, however, there were family secrets that I could not recall without the help of expert guidance.

A few years ago, I began craniosacral therapy (CST), which is a non-invasive, hands-on therapy that uses touch to "release restrictions of the craniosacral system to improve the functioning of the central nervous system," according to the Upledger Institute. Used for a variety reasons, CST helped me with post-traumatic stress from childhood. Through that therapy, I was able to uncover memories from my past, even having been kicked while in the womb of my mother. Hank had given me alcohol, because he thought it was funny when I got tipsy. Even when I was two and a half years old, he would discipline me, unnecessarily, when I couldn't use a fork to pick up string beans.

Turns out, his dad always done that to him, and Hank had hated it. But he was passing it along to me.

I have other memories of Hank beating my mother in front of me. I would try to wrap around his leg to stop him from hurting her, but he would shake me off so he could keep charging at my mom.

DOMESTIC, SEXUAL, AND CHILD ABUSE—Regardless of the age, physical abuse occurs when physical force is used against you in a way that injures or endangers you. Physical assault and battery are crimes, whether they occur inside or outside of a family. Any situation in which you are forced to participate in unwanted, unsafe, or degrading sexual activity is sexual abuse. Forced sex, even by a spouse or intimate partner with whom you also have consensual sex, is an act of aggression and domestic violence.

After the playground incident, breaking my arm, and putting my face between Hank's fist and my mom's face (see Introduction), my uncle helped move us out. My mother went into hiding, fearing the worst from Hank, while I eventually moved to be raised by my Hungarian grandmother in Wheaton, Maryland.

A suburb of Washington, D.C., Wheaton is populated with a lot of immigrant families. As you recall, my grandmother had a troubled childhood, which made her paranoid, particularly about sex. For example, while a mere five-year-old, I would overhear her instructing my uncle, who was eleven years older than me, to "stay away from girls, because all they want is to get pregnant and trap you for the rest of your life."

She walked us to school every day, reminding us, "Don't talk to strangers, because they're always trying to sleep with you, or they're trying to kidnap you or take you away. Strangers are bad. People are bad. You can't trust anybody."

While Hank was away, his mother (my Italian grandmother) would make a point to spend time with us, often on holidays or other occasions. Naturally, she was always on Hank's side, saying to us, "Your mom is terrible. She's a Hungarian witch. Your dad is the best, and he loves you so much," and blah, blah, blah.

"Okay, but where is he?" I finally said, because he was never around at Christmas. Birthdays were combined onto one card, and we never received any gifts. Hank would tell us how he cared about us, but rarely were we with him, much less under his paternal security.

From the time he left until I was eighteen years old, I saw him maybe five times. During that time, my Italian grandmother tried to alienate us from our mother with all kinds of manipulation. It continued an abusive pattern that I had seen throughout my lifetime, but I never put much stock in what she said, because I knew she was lying.

Meanwhile, my parents divorced, and Hank moved to California, because at the time California did not require spouses to pay child support or alimony. Still, around third grade, my mother managed to move us out of our grandparents' home and into an affordable-housing apartment—aka "the projects"—where we were the only white kids I knew of. We went from an immigrant neighborhood to being the only white kids in the projects.

My multi-cultural background gave me eyes that do not see color, but other aspects of the environment were hard to miss. For example, one morning my brother and I found a male body floating in our project's swimming pool. We started throwing things at him, because we were just kids. Turns out, he was dead. We would also play "Count the Cockroaches" every morning, where we open up the cabinet door and count how many cockroaches we could see.

During that time, I was becoming desensitized to massive trauma. But I was also becoming more sensitive to mass—a faith in God as my ultimate father.

My grandparents would cart us off every Saturday to confession, and every Sunday to mass. At one point, the priest spoke about God being the father to the fatherless. That was hope I had never heard, because I didn't have a biological father anymore. I had found something at church that I no longer had in my life. Yet, as a seven-year-old, I was playing the hoodlum in school and not really paying attention to right and wrong. I would lie to the priest during confession time, making up stories so I wouldn't have to confess the real stuff. Eventually, God's love and grace won me over, and my spiritual life awakened.

MOVING UP, BUT NOT AWAY FROM ABUSE

During that time, and through lots of hard work, juggling family and career, my mother found a really good job. When her boss learned of the squalor we lived in, without child support, he bought a house in a cute, little suburb called Rockville, Maryland. He rented the house to us for the same amount that we paid to live in the project. So, we went from a really rough part of town to Suburbia, USA.

Instead of being the bully with a gang around me, I became the weaker target of bullying, largely because my mom was single, and everybody else had a mom and a dad. That weird prejudice was heavy, because we didn't fit into the mold. So, I became the class clown, the talker of the classroom who cracked jokes. I was also covering up dyslexia, which made schoolwork all the more difficult for me. My grades suffered.

Soon, my mother's relationship with her boss became more than platonic and professional. They married, and when I was twelve, we moved from suburbia to the wealthiest neighborhood in Potomac, Maryland, near Washington, D.C. The Marriott family were our neighbors, with the head of the Church of Jesus Christ of Latter-day Saints across the street. Senator John Glenn lived down the road, along with a former governor from Pennsylvania, the secretary of defense, and brain surgeons, among other influential people. That was a big change from counting cockroaches and using a floating dead body for target practice.

The new lifestyle, while looking and sounding great, was not an easy for me to adjust to. I knew I would have to adapt again. My mother's husband, Lee, was certainly generous. So, my brother and I agreed to Lee adopting us.

With a new dad, a new home, a new neighborhood, a new school, and new friends, you'd think I would have been happily on my way to being a teenager. But those past traumas stacked up, never went away, and were never dealt with. My own psychological problems kicked in, and I stopped eating, to the point of reaching anorexia, but my parents wouldn't acknowledge that until my doctor did.

My new dad, Lee, although charming and wonderful in many ways, was also narcissistic, with lots of obsessive-compulsive disorder (OCD) traits that made living with him incredibly difficult. The house had to be white-glove spotless, with nothing on the floors, and everything had to be in its place for Lee. If not, it was always our fault. There were rules for everything: How we ate, who we associated with, where we went, how we dressed, how we talked and what we did.

NARCISSISTIC PERSONALITY DISORDER—A condition characterized by disproportionately deriving gratification from admiring one's own mental or physical attributes. Sufferers are unusually self-involved and show a constant need for admiration, a lack of empathy for others, and a grandiose sense of self-importance.

I couldn't help but feel like an outsider, after all, I went from making my own rules up as a bully to having to follow strict society guidelines. I felt lost, and abandoned, yet again. So, I returned to the one place I had found peace and balance: Church.

At my insistence, we went from one church to another until we landed at National Presbyterian Church in Washington, D.C. That church is like the cathedral for all Presbyterians. President Ronald Reagan went to church with us. I would get to know lots of powerful people, such as senators, congressmen, and judges, because we went to church together. Regardless of who attended, that's where my faith really started to grow.

Although my faith had found a place to be planted, my home life suffered from having a narcissistic dad. It was his way or the highway, and he frequently reminded us of this. When I challenged this concept, his intimidating stare and sharp disapproval was followed up with long durations of silent treatment. We didn't take any real vacations together, because all of our trips were centered around activities that our dad wanted to do. It was rarely about my brother or me—we were just along for the ride.

Living with my dad was like trying to measure up to his highest standards every day, and knowing you will fail. He would remind me that I was never good enough, especially compared with what he had accomplished. Whatever I did in life, he always had done that, and better. I just couldn't measure up to who he was, which meant that I was always beneath him at some level.

He liked it that way.

At that point in time, I excelled at playing piano and winning competitions. I could play forty pages of music from memory. I was playing concertos and all kinds of stuff, no small potatoes.

My mom would be proud and brag about me. Not my dad. He would say, "Yeah, but you know, she failed her biology class." With everything I did, there was "Yeah, but . . . ." He would knock me down a couple notches, so that I couldn't ever enjoy something or take pride in what I had done.

He would say, "I'm just trying to keep you humble." That was his line. For a kid who already struggled with a sense of identity, that wasn't helpful.

At that point, I needed encouragement to grow, with guidance and leadership. I'd shown signs of leadership, but I needed a mentor who would lift me up. Instead, I was always being put down, and I was always under his control. That continued through high school. I learned to deal with it, but couldn't wait to graduate and move on to college.

LEARNING BY EXPERIENCE

Unlike everyone else in my family, who had gone to the University of Maryland, I chose James Madison University, where I became a wild child. Free from the home-related and faith restrictions, I wanted to party, drink, try drugs, and do everything else you're not supposed to do. Nobody was telling me what to do, with lots of rules to follow anymore, like how to talk or eat, whom to hang out with, or even what clothes to wear. College gave me opportunities to experience life without a tether to my controlling parents.

At one party, however, I wish had remembered my mother's and grandmother's warnings.

While hanging out at a fraternity, there was a rugby player I knew, named Danny. He had returned to school after a six-month layoff on crutches, with his leg in a cast. We started talking, and he finally asked me, "Hey, can you help me take my books back to my dorm room?"

"Sure." He seemed like a nice enough guy, but I didn't know him that well. I helped him back to his dorm room, and before entering, I had a bad feeling and thought, *I shouldn't go into his bedroom.*

"Please, just put the books over there on my desk—it would really help a lot," he said. Dismissing my intuition, he closed the door behind me. As I turned around, he raised his crutches as weapons and use his leg cast to force me down on the bed, where he raped me. He stayed on top, pinning me down for a few hours while he slept. Finally, in the wee hours of the morning, I was able to slide out of bed and out of his room. As the door closed behind me, I heard him screaming and shouting for his suite-mate to stop me from leaving. I ran back to my dorm room and I did what many rape victims do. I walked straight into the shower, fully dressed, and just sobbed under the water. Then I took off my clothes and threw them in the trash can and waited for somebody to come offer me a towel.

At that moment, I decided that I could bury this. I chose to open this little box in my brain, put the memory in, close the box and seal it. I told myself, *I'm never going to talk about it ever again.* I didn't report the incident, because I feared a similar backlash like another girl who had been raped had received. They trashed her name, blaming her for the rape.

Shortly after that, I met Peter.

Rape damages women at their core. Left stuffed inside, it warps decision-making and self-esteem. That's probably why I chose Peter to be my husband out of school, instead of a more responsible human being.

Like my dad, Lee, Peter is every bit the narcissist, and like Hank, he became abusive toward me. He would leave for days at a time, returning with random and ridiculous stories and behavior, which later turned out to be excuses for his affair. Still, I didn't leave him for two main reasons: First, I still hoped for something better for our marriage. Second, Peter's brother, Henry, threatened me that, if I ever were to leave Peter, he would kill me. "It's not a matter of if, it's a matter of when. I will hunt you down, and I will find you. And when you think you're safe, I will kill you."

I managed to keep the rape a secret for several years, until Peter and I were having dinner with one of his friends. The friend was rude, crass, and a real ass. At one point, he said at the dinner table, "Women who get raped deserve it." All of the memory of the rape crashed open the box in my brain. I felt nauseous and ran to the bathroom to throw up.

It was as if I was experiencing the after-effects all over again. I couldn't stop shaking and crying. I was a mess. I had suppressed the memory to the point where I had forgotten about it. I had put it out of my mind for so long. But something was happening in the process.

My whole life started to make sense. During that moment of clarity, I asked myself, *Why was I in this place with that kind of jerk, who thought I deserved to be raped?*

That became a turning point for me, and I started asking questions like *How do I get out of here? How do I get out of this? What have I done?* My eyes were opened to the cycles of abuse that I had virtually inherited from my mother and grandmother, even marrying a man with traits resembling the worst of Lee and Hank.

I took a full look around my life, and I asked myself, *Who have I married? And what am I doing? Where am I?*

This pursuit of answers led me back to a relationship with God. I decided that I was done messing around with my life and playing with my faith. That was when God opened my eyes and allowed me to see things, helping me to get out at the right time and the right place.

Soon, Peter suggested we move from Pennsylvania to Florida, where I'd always wanted to live. We made the trek, and after unloading the last box in our new home in Tampa, Peter said, "Okay, I'm going to return the truck back to New Jersey."

"What do you mean, you're taking the truck back to New Jersey?" I asked incredulously.

"I'll be back in a week. I just have one more business thing I have to do, and then I'll be back."

Well, he didn't come back for six months.

He is the one I wrote about in the Introduction, the one who threw the vase at my head upon his return. I divorced Peter immediately after that and moved on.

Then I met my current husband, Michael. He's an attorney, and he's blessed me with three kids. Plus, he's not a narcissist. He may have his own issues, but that's not one of them. We've grown together, and we've been through a lot.

LEANING INTO A NEW CAREER

Early in my new marriage, I volunteered to offer counseling at First Baptist Orlando. I led pre-marital groups for nearly ten years. It was a natural fit, and more people started coming to me with their problems. The stories increased in difficulty, with lots of abuse and trauma, which I could relate to instinctively, but admittedly I didn't have the education I needed in order to help these people. I felt pulled into this counseling career and began the process of becoming a Licensed Mental Health Counselor. That required getting a master's degree first, then completing numerous internship hours before passing a standardized examination.

During that period, I was either studying, counseling, or teaching. My kids, who were in elementary school, fell a tier on my priorities list, just like what had happened with my mother, my grandmother, and her mother.

I had imagined the life of a licensed counselor to be working with cute little couples who squabble about minor problems. But soon, it was clear that my path would not be so easy. My schedule booked up with narcissists, borderlines, sociopaths, and other really difficult cases. Weirdly enough, that little bullying side of me would serve me when I needed to call a spade a spade. People don't expect that to come out, but when it does, they don't mess with me afterward.

Looking back, I remember many other examples of abuse and trauma that impacted my life. For example, my son almost died at eight days old. At work, I've walked the valley of a passive-aggressive boss who made life miserable, before, during, and after the workday; my husband has sought counseling for anger, verbal abuse, and manipulating truth to fit his narrative; my father Lee developed Alzheimer's late in life and began using me as a verbal whipping tool. But these days, I have a new outlook: There's hope for healing when abuse is identified.

MAJOR ABUSE PATTERNS

From my story, you can find lots of possible ways that my life, from the genetic impact on my biology, along with environmental conditioning, has been affected by abuse. Here are a few of the highlights:

Before Conception

- Grandmother's paranoia about sex. Unsettled upbringing until convent. Workaholic.
- Grandmother's father had Spanish flu and died. Spent early childhood in orphanages and foster homes, living in poor conditions.
- Major move from Hungary to America at twelve.
- Living on the run from the Russians.
- Grandfather brought an entitlement from our nobility, and roots in Hungarian life.
- Mother was born as bombs exploded nearby.
- Mother spent early years displaced in America in poor living conditions. Grandfather worked three jobs and was absent.
- Major move from New York City to Indiana at age nine.
- Immigrant family.

Prenatal

- Mother's fear. Workaholic. Mother being abused by husband.
- Hearing my father yelling at mother, and felt being kicked.

Ages 2–5

- Observing my mother being beaten. Bringing her my stuffed animals to console her and yelling at my dad to stop hurting her.
- Breaking my arm. Intercepting—with my own face—my dad's attempt to punch my mom.

- Due to my mother being away, being raised by my grandmother, who taught us about "family secrets" and avoiding men.
- Like grandmother and mother, also had absent father.

Age 5–11

- Being bullied at school. Becoming a bully at my new school.
- Parental alienation by my Italian grandmother with constant badmouthing of my mother.
- Keeping family secrets, and suppressing feelings of hurt and pain.
- Moving around, living in poor conditions.

Ages 12–17

- Major move from lower middle class to upper class, at twelve years old (just like my grandmother).
- Toxicity of living with over-controlling, narcissistic dad who had OCD; never getting anything right. Surprise trips that led to insecurity.
- Developed anorexia, anxiety, and fears (just like my grandmother).

Ages 17–21

- Self-harming with alcohol and drug abuse.
- Raped in college by a fellow student.

20s

- I married an abusive narcissist, like Hank. I was abandoned without financial support, verbally abused, and cheated on (just like my mother). My life was threatened.
- Early in my adulthood, I mistreated numerous friends and lost many friendships due to my behavior.

30s and Older

- Second husband could flip into rage during an argument. My son would also be verbally abusive to his sister.

- Sexual harassment—by both men and women—at almost every job I've had.
- A cyberstalker would leave disturbing comments in my social media.
- Bosses have bullied, belittled, lied, undermined my progress, and taken credit for my work.
- Two clients of mine have given me death threats, and another committed a felony against me.
- At church, I've been ostracized by church members and leadership for not automatically falling in line with leadership.
- Another time, while working as a therapist, I had to report an abuse to the Florida Department of Children and Family Services (DCF) but was "penalized" for not handling it within the church.

While I have more examples, when I add all these events together, it's easy to see that I can relate to all kinds of abuse. But more importantly, there's a theme—a pathology—that runs through my family. Here are some traits that have been passed down:

- **Paranoia**: "People outside the family are trying to destroy me." "I can't trust authorities."
- **Anxiety**: Constant worrying about what could happen, thinking the worst, and planning for it mentally. Everyone in my family has generalized anxiety disorder (GAD).
- **Secretive behavior**: Keeping secrets in the family; not disclosing information or abuse to friends or family members.
- **Pride**: "I can handle it." "I don't need help from others."
- **Denial**: "It's not that bad." "Everyone has issues."
- **Arrogance**: "I'm not like those other people who get abused." "I'm better than that." "I'm too smart for that."
- **Adaptability**: "I can survive anything." "I have a long family history of survivors."

- **Loyalty**: When "family is everything," or "We don't betray the family or talk badly about them." This loyalty can justify not reporting abusive behavior.
- **Courageous**: Taking bold action when the children are threatened, while avoiding the adult's, or parent's, own issues that may have caused the problems.
- **Hardworking**: Hard work sounds like a great characteristic, but not when it consumes the individual so their life becomes out of balance, like a workaholic.
- **Faith**: In the background, throughout my family is a commitment to faith. Whether or not everyone actually believed will be known in the afterlife.

Not all of these are necessarily "bad," but they can have a flip side when overdone.

IN THE MIDDLE

From the first punch I received or threw, I've naturally wanted to get in between abusers and victims, protect the victim and stop the abuser. This instinct of mine follows me everywhere—from the grocery store parking lots to my office couch, where families regularly come for me to referee a discussion. Now, I can usually identify the abuse even before the client does. I've seen so much abuse and trauma that I can sense the causes of disappointment, depression, anxiety, betrayal, and many other symptoms of abuse.

I gravitate toward abusers and their victims. In many ways, when I work with them, I am sticking my head between them and trying to stop the abuse. I have seen abusers of all types: men who are angry with their wives, parents who abuse their children, women who are angry with their husbands, hidden abuse in churches (with attempts to cover it up), children who are abusive to their parents, teenagers who are abusive to their friends, retirees who are abusive to their spouses, and teens or adults who self-abuse through alcohol, rage, or drugs.

When I face an abusive situation, I turn off all emotion, and I become cold, eerily calm, quiet, and hyper-vigilant. I can feel my heart rate lowering, my breathing becoming deeper and more intentional, and my senses come alive as if looking for stimulation. All expression leaves my face, and I scan the environment for potential escapes, weapons, and potential threats.

My thinking is hyper-focused as I work out possible scenarios, as if playing a game of chess. I do this when I'm in client sessions, at home, or even at a store. It is as if my senses are keenly aware of abuse. But that doesn't mean I always step in. Sometimes, to de-escalate the event, I need to do nothing or step back. Other times, I do step in verbally or physically. But regardless of the situation, my focus is on the physical safety of the victim.

Although we grew up in different decades, there are patterns that have seemed to reassert themselves, from my grandmother to my mother to me. Ironically, these patterns have given me the ability to fight back against the abuse in my own life. It's taken years, but now I am more than equipped with experience and expertise to shed light, and heal the wounds from abuse.

That's why this book had to be written—for myself, my children, and the lives of others I come into contact with.

REWRITING MY STORY

My journey sometimes feels as though I'm wandering in the desert, stumbling onto wells of oasis every now and then. While suffering and surviving a wild childhood, abusive marriages, and more, today I can look back and see a purpose through it all. For me, I've been an apprentice to abuse from before day one. It's in my family history and my strong-willed personality. It has been passed down from my mother and grandmother and has given me a chance to rewrite my story and many others' stories as well.

Your life looks different from mine, but abuse is a part of it to some degree. We all have been infected by the abuse virus, but we don't all have to succumb to it. Today, I don't gloss over the abuse in my story. I'm openly sharing because I am healing from the past. I've seen others who have been on the same journey. It's not about righting wrongs. Instead, it's taking responsibility for our own roles—even as the victims—and being able to identify abuse sooner than later. My story was written to save lives. It wasn't an easy journey, but it brought me here. Now I can help stop abuse in its tracks, and you can, too.

FACTS (OLD STORY)	NEW STORY
I was a victim of abuse.	Abuse is in my past, but it does not define me.
I was hurt by abuse I didn't even realize.	I've learned that I can stop the abuse in my life.
I hurt others.	My past helps me help others.
I made bad decisions.	I learned to adapt and work hard with balance.

Chapter Two

Warning Signs

O ur brains are gifted with an ability to have a feeling about someone or something. It's called "intuition." In the largest study of its kind, comparing more than 46,000 brain scans, neuroscientists found that women have more activity in the area of the brain that controls intuition than men do.[10] Still, man or woman, you may have a funny feeling right now, and maybe you can't describe it. Maybe you already know that you are being abused and/or have been abused, or aren't sure whether there has been abuse, but you need to discover the path that led you where you are today. In this chapter, I outline several warning signs, both intuitive and factual, that can help you begin to trace the steps of abuse.

---

10. Amen D.G., Trujillo M., Keator D., Taylor D.V., Willeumier K., Meysami S, Raji C.A. "Gender-Based Cerebral Perfusion Differences in 46,034 Functional Neuroimaging Scans." *Journal of Alzheimer's Disease*. 2017; 60(2): 605–14. doi: 10.3233/JAD-170432. PMID: 28777753.

Many types of abuse exist, and we'll cover many of them in Chapter 5. If the situation you are experiencing puts you in danger, that's an obvious sign that you are being abused. However, even the feeling of being in danger can be a warning sign. Anxiety is the emotional precursor to fear. Think of it as the low-fuel light in your car—a warning that if you don't get gas soon, your car will run out. Your current anxiety might be a warning sign that you are experiencing abuse.

The first step is to become aware that something is not right, helpful, or healthy. That requires becoming aware of our thoughts and feelings without rejecting them, as the abuser would have it. A victim must become aware of their environment without judgment, identifying true feelings of love, joy, and trust instead of hate, sadness, and fear. Without awareness, we remain foggy, unable to see a clear path. You might not be able to see all the steps, but you can manage the next one: owning it.

OWNING IT

The next step is to acknowledge we have a role in our situation. How? Instead of focusing on the external, look inward. The thoughts we tell ourselves can lead to unhealthy behaviors that place us in problematic situations. Let me give you a few examples:

- **Inner critic:** Telling yourself, "I'm not good enough" or "I will always be a failure." Soon, your brain begins to believe what you're telling yourself and will find ways to sabotage you instead of helping you succeed.
- **Obsessive thinking:** Repeatedly thinking about the same thing or incident over and over, leading to no different outcome. It is often used to punish oneself for poor choices, which can lead us to seek relationships that put us in the blaming seat.
- **Stuffing (Suppressing) emotions:** "I shouldn't feel this way" and "My feelings don't matter" are dangerous signs, because continued emotional stuffing often leads to explosive, uncharacteristic outbursts later, which can destroy relationships.

- **Dangerous attractions:** "I can handle them" is a common lie we tell ourselves, putting us in dangerous situations without taking safety precautions. It can lead us to engage in harmful or abusive relationships or activities that can destroy our lives.
- **Addiction and abuse:** "I want to forget" leads to escaping reality and numbing the mind and body through a wide variety of means, including drugs (prescription and/or illegal), sex, alcohol, exercise, shopping, gaming, the Internet, social media, gambling, smoking, sugar, caffeine, work, and food.
  - Abuse of a substance is different from a dependency; the two can co-exist, but one is not necessarily an indication of the other. However, both are destructive to the brain, body, and relationships.

- **Self-inflicted pain:** Your behaviors that hurt you can be warning signs of being abused or being able to abuse others. Watch for hitting yourself (e.g., in the head), throwing yourself against a wall, cutting, picking, burning, ingesting toxic substances, carving words or symbols on your skin, unnecessary scratching, piercing your skin with sharp objects, pulling hair, or picking at wounds. These behaviors often lead to social isolation and loneliness.
- **Eating disorders:** "I need to be in control of something" is a common sentiment when life seems out of control. Eating is natural for humans, but when there has been abuse, or related fears, sometimes food is the either the first or last thing people think about. Eating, or avoiding eating food, can be a way to cope with the conflict. That may include overeating, bulimia, anorexia, binging, pica (eating things that are not considered food), rumination (chewing, spitting out, re-chewing), and highly-restrictive dieting—all of which can be life-threatening.
- **Depression and suicidal ideation/parasuicide:** "I'm never going to feel better" is what we may tell ourselves when hope is lost.

25

Depression should be treated like an emergency condition. It's a slippery slope that can lead to thinking about ending your own life. Depression can be a consequence of previous, or hidden, abuse.

If you feel depressed to the point of thinking about suicide, and are not being treated by a professional such as a physician or therapist, please contact the National Suicide Prevention Hotline: (toll free) 800-273-8255.

Each one of these thoughts leads to potentially dangerous behaviors. But how does that happen?

Often, we adopt our own "distorted thinking" from our abuser. One of the many consequences of abusive behavior is a change in the victim's thinking patterns. After years of badgering, the victim finally adopts the abuser's distorted reasoning. In many cases, the victim does not become an abuser. Rather, as they attempt to minimize further abuse, their survivor instincts take over in anticipation of the next attack, and they begin to think like their abuser.

If any of the following common phrases sounds familiar, it could be because the abuser says or said these things, and the abusive situation(s) taught you to think that way. These concepts and phrases are written about further by Dr. David Burns in *Ten Days to Self-Esteem*.

All-or-nothing thinking: Do you see only in black or white, in absolute categories? This can include the following: "I am always late." "I never do anything right." "Every time I try to do this. . . " "If I lose this, I lose it all."

Overgeneralization: Do you see a negative event as never ending? This can include the following: "This bullying will never end." "I'm stuck forever." "These people always . . . ."

Mental filter: Do you dwell on the negative and filter out the positive? For example, in one day you might receive five compliments and one criticism on your appearance. Do you only focus on the one negative remark and disregard all the positive ones?

Discounting the positives: Do you insist that your accomplishments and positive inputs don't count? This can include the following: "My accomplishments don't matter." "They gave me that award out of pity."

Remember when I mentioned that intuition can go a bit too far?

- **Mind-reading:** Do you assume that people are reacting negatively to you? This can include the following: "I just know they think I'm stupid." "They must be thinking badly about me."
- **"Fortune-telling":** Do you predict things will turn out badly? This can include the following: "There is no way they will like my idea." "I just know this will never work."

Magnification or minimization: Do you blow things out of proportion or minimize their significance? Magnification is making a mountain out of a molehill, and minimization is making a molehill out of a mountain.

Emotional reasoning: Do you reason from how you feel? This can include the following: "I feel dumb, so I must be." "I feel guilty, so I must be guilty of something."

"Should" statements: Do you criticize yourself and others with "should," "shouldn't," "must," "have to," and "ought"? Do you say, "I should have done that"? "You must do this or else"?

Labeling: Do you attach a harsh label to yourself after you have made a mistake? This can include the following: "I'm a loser." "I'm a fool."

Blame: Do you blame yourself for something you weren't responsible for, or do you blame others? This can include the following: "It's my fault that you are married." "You are to blame for my marriage falling apart."

Once the destructive thinking has been identified, counteract it with the truth. Ask yourself questions like: "Are you really *always* to blame?" "Were you ever on time?" "Do you really *have to* do that?" Then replace the negative statement with a positive one. "I'm a fool" could be replaced with "I'm wise in this other area." This is the beginning of learning how to rewrite your story.

LIES ABUSERS TELL VICTIMS

After we've recognized these statements as having a negative impact on your life, we can turn to the warning signs that are offered up by abusers. The most common are lies. Abusers lie to their victims to cover up, manipulate, and misdirect. The saddest part is that abusers take advantage of the trust and love from their victims. What do abusers say to their victims to get them to acquiesce? Let's listen to the lies that abusers tell their victims. Some of the statements listed below might even sound acceptable in certain environments, but they are not. Abusive behavior is pervasive, and without awareness, it will continue.

If any of these sounds familiar, I encourage you to jot them down in your journal as a reference for your new story.

Common Lies and Statements Abusers Tell Victims

Power

"I only hurt you because you hurt me first."

"I do this (abuse) because I love you."

"Your family or friends can't be trusted, you can only trust me."

"You are such a (degrading name)."

"No one will ever love you like I do."

"The Bible says you have to have sex with me, so do it."

"I am an example for the whole church, so you have to behave perfectly."

Control

"You never do what I ask."

"Just do it my way, and everything will be fine."

"I know what is best for you; your judgment is off."

"This (abuse) is for your own good."

"If you don't have sex with me, then I'll have to have it with someone else."

"I'm in control of you, even at work."

"It's not stealing when it's family."

"I'm perfect, and you have to be, as well."

"You don't hear me when I talk in a normal voice."

Intimidation

"You make me feel so angry."

"I'll talk to you when you have done what I asked."

"I'm stronger/more powerful/smarter than you."

"You should be ashamed of yourself; I'm not like that at all."

"I have to hit you to get your attention."

Manipulation

"If only you would (do something), then I wouldn't have to react badly."

"This is our little secret—no one needs to know."

"You misheard me—I would never say that."

"I will hurt myself if you leave me."

"I have to have sex, and it's your duty to give it to me."

"Just do this one (sexually degrading) thing one time, and then I'll be satisfied."

"A good wife or husband would do this for me."

"I'm the one who feels (angry); you can't feel that way."

"If you don't do this, I'll leave (divorce) you."

"When you (do something), then I'll have sex with you."

"I lied to protect you."

"You have to submit to me. God said so."

"You intentionally make up stories about me to embarrass me."

Isolation

"You have a bad memory. I know what really happened."

"It is your fault that we are in this mess, not mine."

"You don't deserve the things I give you."

"When you start being nice to me, then I will give you a birthday gift."

"You're confused; I know what is right."

"You can't manage money, so I have to keep you out of the accounts."

"If you don't follow this (religious rule), then you will be kicked out."

"It's not my fault that you are hypersensitive."

"No one could forgive you for what you have done."

"This (abuse) is a family matter; no one needs to know about it."

Spot one that sounds too familiar? May two or more? You're not alone. These are warning signs of potential trouble. But it doesn't have to escalate further. A licensed counselor or therapist who specializes in abuse can walk you through the process safely. I've also included several resources in the back of the book.

DECEPTIVE EXCUSES FOR ABUSIVE BEHAVIOR

Abusers are experts at using deceptive excuses for their behavior, similar to outright lies. They can justify anything, because they cannot, or will not, accept responsibility for their own words and behaviors. It's almost always someone else's fault.

Here's an example that may ring a few bells. Brandon is a great guy. He is detail-oriented, he works hard, and cares about his family. But he brings abusive traits from his mother, who was domineering, manipulative, and controlling, among other abusive traits. Because Brandon did not acknowledge and work through these abuses, he wound up marrying a woman with very similar traits, putting him in the exact scenario he was raised in. His wife was effective at verbal and mental abuse—gaslighting—twisting the truth to fit her cause. She controlled the money, preventing him access to bank accounts and records, so he didn't know what was going on financially. After a while, his children turned on him, because he worked a lot, but they also were listening to their mother, who would share half-truths and lies to win them over. Brandon trusted his wife and believed the words she dished out at him. Beaten down, confused, hazy, and exhausted, he sought help from a therapist. At first, he could not comprehend that he was the victim of abuse. He believed the lies that he was to blame. He thought abuse was only physical. But then Brandon learned that it could also be verbal, emotional, mental, sexual, spiritual, and/or financial.

One muscle that Brandon had to exercise was to learn not to accept the excuses given to justify the abusers' behaviors. We made a list, evaluated each item individually, and changed his perspective so he could refuse to absorb the tossed responsibility. Here are some examples:

1. **"I'm sorry, but . . . "** Any apology that ends with "but" is not a real apology. Rather, it is an attempt to pass the blame onto the other person while not fully accepting responsibility. A true apology is expressed with remorse and doesn't point the finger. There is no "but" at the end of it.

2. **"It's all your fault . . . "** Blame-shifting is a common tactic that abusive people use to deflect their behavior. By pointing out some minor infraction done by the other person, they justify their abusiveness. It's also done to avoid responsibility, admitting to doing wrong, or having to see things from a different perspective.

3. **"You are so much like . . . "** This statement is typically followed by the name of a person whom either the abuser or the abused despises. The idea is that by saying the victim is acting similar to a distasteful person, the abuser is absolved for their behavior. It is also a way of making the abuser superior to the inferior victim.

4. **"You triggered me . . . "** While the statement could be truthful, using past trauma as justification for future abuse is not acceptable. Victims who want to heal use their triggers to identify potential negative reactions so they can get better, not

so they can continue to harm others. Being triggered is not a valid excuse for taking advantage of someone.

5. **"You make me so angry . . . "** Here's a thought: Why do you want to be around someone who makes you angry? No one can "make" another person angry; at some point, the choice to emote is a decision. But if someone is constantly antagonistic, why be with them? Clearly, the relationship is not on a positive track.

6. **"If you treated me with more respect . . . "** Respect is earned over time, it cannot be commanded instantly. People who demand respect often don't deserve it. Respect should be given in the same measure it is received. Abusive behavior is not justified because of a lack of respect. It does nothing to gain respect, and everything to lose it.

7. **"If you didn't react that way . . . "** This is another form of blame-shifting where the victim's responses are used to acquit the abuser. Most victims find that even when they modify their reactions, the abuser still does the same thing. It becomes a never-ending shifting of expectations designed to keep the victim on their toes.

8. **"Because you don't listen to me, I had to . . . "** Instead of trying to find calmer ways of addressing an issue, the abuser uses this as an opportunity to escalate. There are any number of reasons why a person might not be listening, and trying to force the matter does not make things better. This is punishment, similar to the way a parent speaks to a child.

9. **"If you hadn't done . . . "** This is another combination of shifting the blame by highlighting a flaw in the other person. The underlying manipulation is calculated to impose a parent/child relationship where the abuser is the authoritarian, and the victim is needing correction. Once again, the abuser becomes superior, and the victim inferior.

10. **"Your words hurt me so . . . "** There is an old saying, "Hurt people hurt people." But even if a person is hurt by a statement,

they are still responsible for how they react afterward. Being hurt is not an excuse for abusive behavior.

11. **"My whole family is this way . . . "** By assigning blame to their family of origin, the abuser minimizes their actions as collective behavior. Because everyone in the family does it, then it is OK to continue abusing.

12. **"It's in the blood . . . "** Instead of using abusive behavior as a means for deciding to change, the abuser says it's part of their personality, or someone in their family is the same way. That allows the abuser to escape responsibility and assign responsibility to a parent or culture. Again, everyone is responsible for their own behavior.

13. **"You won't take me seriously, so I had to . . . "** Abusers are generally dichotomous thinkers; things are either one extreme way or another. There is no middle ground to them. So, when the victim minimizes a statement, they are forced to overreact instead of finding an alternative solution. This is a no-win situation for the victim.

14. **"You brought this on yourself . . . "** This is another version of blame-shifting with an added twist of fortune-telling responsibility. By saying the victim should have predicted the abuse and avoided the subject, once again, abusers absolve themselves. It is a clever way to cast blame.

15. **"You know what sets me off . . . "** Everyone can be set off by something. Anger is a normal and healthy response during grieving when a person feels violated or taken advantage of, or even when someone they love is being harmed. Abusers, however, use their anger to abuse others.

16. **"If you weren't such a *#@^% . . . "** Name-calling is abusive behavior by itself. It demoralizes a person while elevating the abuser to superior status. Using it instead of apologizing widens the gap further. Don't tolerate this behavior from anyone.

17. **"You're just being sensitive . . . "** For the record, being sensitive is a gift, not a curse. This statement takes the positive traits of the victim and turns them into negative ones. It is a reflection of an abuser not valuing the sensitivity of the victim and, instead, making fun of the victim for feeling an emotion.

These statements are lame, false, and deceiving. They are not coming from a place of honesty, love, care, or concern for the other person. If you have ever caught yourself saying any of these phrases, don't worry—we will address them in Chapter 4.

This exercise helped Brandon set new boundaries with his family and leave his abusive wife. Plus, with his newfound knowledge of abuse, he was able to find someone who didn't treat him that way.

The opposite extreme of these abusive statements, is making no statements at all—we call that "the Silent Treatment."

THE SILENT TREATMENT: THE SUBTLE ART OF ABUSE

Another client example, Margo, would intuitively "know" that she must have messed up because her husband would give her the silent treatment. But she didn't know exactly what she had done wrong. Had she drunk too much at her husband's office party and said something embarrassing? Or is he perhaps upset over the new pile on the kitchen counter? Could it be that she had spent too much on groceries, because they are trying to eat healthily? Or did had he seen her sarcastic text message to a friend about how she was in the doghouse with him again? Regardless, he wouldn't talk to her for thirty days at a stretch, even if Margo would say something or ask about the situation. He didn't even talk to her on her birthday. He would completely ignore her. The only time silence would break was when he needed something from her. Normally, Margo would just confess to everything, apologize, and beg him to start talking again. She hated the silence. He would reluctantly accept her remorse, lecture her about the incidents, and then slowly re-engage. Unfortunately, within a couple of weeks, the same cycle would repeat. She came in to see me, because she was blaming herself for the whole thing.

Through therapy, she began to see how he used silence as a way to control her behavior and get her to accept excessive responsibility. Margo decided she had had enough. She was done being treated like a child. At the beginning of their relationship, she saw his uncommunicativeness as sophistication; eventually, she saw it as manipulation.

Silent Abuse: Examples

- **Ignoring:** Giving a person the "cold shoulder," or ignoring them, is done by dismissing them or even disregarding their existence. It is used as a way to devalue a person and establish a hierarchy of superiority in favor of the abuser. Examples include paying no attention to a person as if they were not present, discounting a comment as if it were not heard, forgetting about an event as if it were never scheduled, or looking down on a person as if they were stupid.
- **Evading:** Instead of flat-ignoring a person, an abuser might evade, stonewall, or shirk communication. This is done by giving one-word answers to open-ended questions, refusing to look in the eyes of a person when they are talking, giving vague responses when asked for specifics, mumbling under their breath, or avoiding giving a response by changing the subject. An abuser uses these tactics to render a conversation meaningless and cause the victim to feel dismissed.
- **Subverting:** This is done to undermine a person's power and put them in a state of destabilization where they are unsure of themselves. Examples include not acknowledging quality work, blindly removing areas of responsibility, resetting expectations without informing, or quietly sabotaging any success. In most cases, this is done in a cunning and crafty way, such that the victim is unaware of the shift until it is too late to handle.

- **Rejecting:** In an intimate relationship, physical refusal of affection is a subtle form of rejection. This can be done non-verbally by pulling away from touch, turning a cheek when being kissed, moving farther away when physically close, and not responding to hugs. It also includes not engaging in sexual behavior with the other person, minimizing the importance of sexual contact, and snubbing any type of intimacy. *Note: If a person has felt abused by their partner, it is normal not to engage in sexual activity with them until healing has occurred.*

- **Quarantining:** Quarantining or isolating is a form of physical and mental abuse where a person's social activity is intentionally restricted. This is done to cut them off from family who might rescue them from their abuser. An abuser refuses to engage with extended family in order to limit where the victim has access. Then the separation is justified by saying, "They don't like me," "They are trying to destroy our relationship," or "They don't really care about you." This subtly expands the silent treatment to include the unknowing participants of the victim's family.

- **Shunning:** Taken to the next level, shunning involves isolation from an entire community. In this case, an organization, religion, or group of friends is both knowingly and unknowingly engaging in the silent treatment. The abuser accomplishes this by going to the group of individuals and spreading lies or rumors about the victim. Usually, the statements demonstrate an inconsistency with the belief system of the group. For instance, the abuser might say to a religious organization that the victim no longer believes in God or that their behavior is not consistent with that of a believer. That puts the victim in a defensive position from which they cannot recover easily.

Understanding the different silent-treatment abuse tactics was the beginning of the end for Margo's relationship with her husband. Once she fully understood how he had manipulated her, her family, and her friends, she decided to leave him. Surprisingly, they had an amicable divorce, almost as though he had been waiting for it for a while. Once divorced, he was nice to her, without any animosity. This showed me that sometimes leaving an abusive marriage can lead to a better result for everyone.

DANGER SIGNS OF ABUSE TURNING DEADLY

Abuse has a pattern similar to addiction. The abuser can become addicted to, or even aroused by, their own misbehaviors, while the victim can actually develop a tolerance for abuse, so it no longer has the same effect. That aggravates the abuser, which then escalates the situation.

In the escalation, the abuser can become more obsessive, intense, erratic, and dangerous. Knowing what to look for can be the difference between life and death.

Watch for these signs, some of which are taken from Gavin De Becker's book *The Gift of Fear*. The abuser can be male or female, from any socioeconomic group or demographic, and can have a variety of traumas in their history.

1. The victim has intuitive feelings that they are in danger.
2. The abuser resolves conflict with threats, intimidation, verbal abuse, bullying, and/or violence. These include threats to harm physically, to defame, to embarrass, to restrict freedom, to disclose secrets, to cut off support, to abandon, and to commit suicide.
3. More than one incident of violent behavior (including vandalism, breaking things, and/or throwing things) has occurred with the abuser. They use symbolic violence (such as tearing a wedding photo or marring a face in it).
4. The abuser has a history of battery in prior relationships.
5. The abuser uses alcohol or drugs, often with adverse effects (such as memory loss, hostility, and/or cruelty).
6. The abuser cites alcohol as an excuse or explanation for hostile or violent conduct. ("That was the booze talking, not me; I got so drunk I was crazy.")

7. The abuser's history includes police encounters for behavioral offenses (such as threats, stalking, assault, and/or battery).

8. The abuser uses money to control the activities, purchases, and behavior of the victim.

9. The abuser becomes jealous of anyone or anything that takes the victim's time away from the relationship, or the abuser keeps the victim on a "tight leash," requiring him or her to account for their time.

10. The abuser projects extreme emotions onto others (such as hate, love, jealousy, and/or commitment) even when there is no evidence that would lead a reasonable person to perceive them.

11. The abuser inappropriately surveils or follows the victim.

12. The abuser suffers severe mood swings or is sullen, angry, or depressed.

13. The abuser refers to weapons as instruments of power, control, or revenge. Weapons are a substantial part of an abuser's persona; the abuser has at least one gun, or they talk about, joke about, read about, and/or collect weapons.

Each of these dangerous indications can lead to deadly consequences. According to the National Institute of Justice, and cited studies, the risk rate of murder-suicide increases when there is:

- Prior history of domestic violence;
- Access to a gun;
- Threats, especially increased threats with increased specificity;
- Prior history of poor mental health and/or substance abuse, especially alcohol.

The National Coalition Against Domestic Violence also reports these statistics[11] (https://ncadv.org/statistics) about homicide:

---

11. National Coalition Against Domestic Violence (2020). Domestic violence. Retrieved from https://assets.speakcdn.com/assets/2497/domestic_violence-2020080709350855.pdf?1596811079991.

- A study of intimate-partner homicides found that 20% of victims were not the intimate partners themselves, but family members, friends, neighbors, persons who intervened, law enforcement responders, or bystanders.
- 72% of all murder-suicides involve an intimate partner; 94% of the victims of these murder-suicides are female.

These statistics are so high because the victims did not pay attention to the warning signs before it was too late.

GROUP PSYCHOLOGICAL ABUSE

The family unit is itself a group, and so far most of what we've covered has involved family-centered abuse. But once we walk out the door, we enter a world made of other groups: at work or church and in gangs, cults, political parties, sororities and fraternities, workout groups, or really any group of people.

Groups typically have a leader who spearheads and organizes the group and usually sets a higher level of expectation than its members have. There may be some type of exclusivity, such as a ritual and/or financial commitment to join. On the surface, everything is fine. But this group is different. Bad behaviors are encouraged, even taught. The behaviors usually escalate quickly, as groups tend to motivate the individuals involved. Those who try to leave, or do leave, the organization are often ostracized, threatened, stalked, and/or tortured. The leader demands complete loyalty, and any deviation from that is punished. Anyone outside of the group who criticizes the organization is treated poorly and/or threatened.

How does the group maintain its membership when outsiders are treated so badly? They use group psychological abuse. Often, it's not obvious, such as a punch to the face, name-calling, guilt-tripping, physical isolation, or neglect. Rather, it is more calculated or even secretive. Sometimes the abuse is conducted within a group setting, which causes the member to feel even more alone and ashamed. Hazing, often an initiation ritual, is an example of this covert group psychological abuse, which gives members a false sense of superiority because they were hazed, too. The group will ostracize anyone who fails the hazing or quits.

This idea of the individual versus a group could happen in a variety of settings. For instance, it could be a new employee entering an established team, a spouse coming into their in-laws' home, or a new believer approaching a church. Whatever the environment, the unit is pre-established with its own set of rules and standards.

Shortly after joining the group, the new member is met with unreasonable expectations and abusive treatment designed to demonstrate that the new person is not part of the group, yet. Instead, the member has to experience several layers of group psychological abuse before they are officially indoctrinated. This is how cults operate, and they are not always religious. Oftentimes, the exterior of a cult is a front for the real deceptive behavior underneath. NXIVM is a recent example that made news, in which the "self-help" group was hiding sex abuse and trafficking. Here are additional true examples:

1. **Indifference:** It didn't matter what Susie said, her comments were returned with a blank stare and an instant change of the subject. Even when she was on point or in agreement, or added a new perspective, she received nothing in return and was treated with disregard.

2. **Discounting:** When John shared how he felt hurt by a remark, he was told, "You shouldn't feel that way." His emotional responses to hurtful statements were discounted, minimized, and villainized to make his behavior look abusive, instead of the group's.

3. **Snubbing:** Angie had not come from the same strict religious background that everyone else had experienced. However, she had grown in her faith and knowledge in the last several years. Yet, whenever she would make a spiritual comment, she was instantly snubbed with silence or the occasional roll of the eyes.

4. **Disinterest:** After spending years with this same group, James realized that the only one who never shared his story was him. As he approached the subject, he was immediately met with disinterest. He still persisted, but as he was speaking, slowly each member got up and physically left the group.

5. **Coldness:** Just by walking into the room, Elizabeth could feel the coldness toward her. She was eight months pregnant, and not one person asked how she was feeling or offered her a place to sit. Everyone else experienced warm greetings and conversation, but she was shunned.

6. **Censorship:** While in the middle of talking about an experience, Matthew was told he could speak no further. "We don't talk about that here" was stated very clearly. His remarks were not inappropriate, however; he was being censored because no one else in the group had the same shared experience.

7. **Exposing:** Mary shared her previous abusive relationship confidentially with one person in the group. At the next gathering, another person made a stabbing remark that clearly indicated that her private information had been exposed to the group without her consent or knowledge.

8. **Ungratefulness:** In an effort to connect with the group, Tom decided to offer his help on a project. Even though he performed the task well, there was no show of thanks. Yet, everyone else who worked on the project, even those who did it grudgingly, received appreciation.

9. **Sarcasm:** Just when Hannah started to feel like a part of the conversation, one person made a sarcastic remark directed at her. The expression on Hannah's face was one of hurt, to which the person replied, "I was only joking." Immediately, she felt isolated from the group yet again.

10. **Denigration:** Over a period of time, it became apparent that Daniel's reputation had been denigrated by the group.

Regardless of the strides he had made, there was a constant air of not forgetting and not forgiving his previous behavior.

Remember, it doesn't matter whether the group does these behaviors at a conscious or subconscious level. It is still hurtful and leads to more abuse. Eventually, the new member realizes the difference and will either try harder to fit in, or leave the organization. This is precisely what the established organization wants. This filtering process ensures that only those who tolerate and respond to abuse remain. This is how the organization knows that its group psychological abuse is effective.

Many times, the group psychological abuse is led by a narcissist. Let's look at the narcissistic cycle of abuse, because it's common in many abusive situations.

THE NARCISSISTIC CYCLE OF ABUSE

The narcissist is able to drive abusive behaviors while justifying them the entire time. It can take a while to realize that the abuse is coming from narcissistic tendencies, because the narcissist is very good at manipulating situations, but a narcissist operates in cycles.

The Cycle of Abuse that Lenore Walker (1979) coined starts with A: tension-building, which is followed by B: acting-out, then C: reconciliation/honeymoon, and completes with D: calm, which is followed again by tension-building and cycles through these stages again.

During tension building, the abuser is looking for opportunities to unleash, while the victim begins to walk on eggshells in anticipation. That leads to an incident where the abuser acts out on the victim. Then, as if the pressure valve has been released, the abuser feels relieved. Seeing the devastation on the victim, they reconcile, saying or doing whatever it takes to appease. Finally, there is a period of calm, or the honeymoon phase, where things seem stable until it happens again. And it does.

CYCLE OF ABUSE

1 TENSIONS BUILDING
Tensions increase, breakdown of communication, victim beaches fearful and feels the need to placate the abuser.

2 INCIDENT
Verbal, emotional & physical abuse. Anger, blaming, arguing. Threats. Intimidation.

4 CALM
Incident is "forgotten," no abuse is taking place. The honeymoon phase

3 RECONCILIATION
Abuser, apologizes, gives excuses, blames the victim, denies the abuse occurred, or says that it wasn't as bad as the victim claims.

Narcissistic Cycle of Abuse

FEELS THREATEN >>> ABUSES OTHERS <<< BECOMES THE VICTIM <<< FEELS EMPOWERED >>>

However, when a narcissist is an abuser, the cycle looks different. The outer circle on the chart above is the typical cycle of abuse with the inner circle demonstrating the narcissistic twist. Narcissism changes the back end of the cycle, because the narcissist is continuously self-centered and unwilling to admit fault. Their need to be superior, right, or in charge limits the possibility of any real reconciliation.

Instead, it is frequently the abused who desperately tries for appeasement while the narcissist plays the victim. This switchback tactic emboldens the narcissist behavior, even more, further convincing them of their faultlessness. Any threat to their authority repeats the cycle.

Here are the four narcissistic cycles of abuse:

1. **Feels Threatened:** An upsetting event occurs, and the narcissist feels threatened. It could be the rejection of sex, disapproval at work, embarrassment in a social setting, jealousy of others' success, or feelings of abandonment, neglect, or disrespect. The abused, aware of the potential threat, becomes nervous. They know that something is about to happen, and they begin to walk on eggshells around the narcissist. Most narcissists repeatedly get upset over the same underlying issues, whether real or imagined. They also tend to obsess about the threat over and over.

2. **Abuses Others:** The narcissist engages in some sort of abusive behavior. The abuse can be physical, mental, verbal, sexual, financial, spiritual, or emotional. It is customized to intimidate the abused in an area of weakness, especially if that area is one of strength for the narcissist. The abuse can last for a few short minutes or as long as several hours. Sometimes a combination of two types of abuse is used. For instance, a narcissist may begin with verbal belittling to wear out the abused, followed by a projection of their lying about an event onto the abused. Finally, tired of the assault, the abused defensively fights back.

3. **Becomes the Victim:** This is when the "switchback" occurs. The narcissist uses the abused behavior as further evidence that they are the one being abused. The narcissist professes their twisted victimization by bringing up past defensive behaviors that the abused has done, as if the abused initiated the abuse. Because the abused has feelings of remorse and guilt, they accept this warped perception and try to rescue the narcissist. This might include giving in to what the narcissist wants,

accepting unnecessary responsibility, placating the narcissist to keep the peace, and agreeing to the narcissistic lies.

4. **Feels Empowered:** Once the abused gives in or gives up, the narcissist feels empowered. This is all the justification the narcissist needs to demonstrate their rightness or superiority. The victim has unknowingly fed the narcissistic ego, only to make it stronger and bolder than before. But every narcissist has an Achilles heel, and the power they feel now will only last until the next threat to their ego appears.

Once the narcissistic cycle of abuse is identified, the victim can plan to escape it at any point. Begin by coming up with strategies for future confrontations, know your limitations, and have a "Plan B" escape plan in place.

Cycles of abuse, generational patterns, and all other warning signs do not need to continue. No one can withstand abuse forever, yet even one act of abuse can leave a scar that lasts a lifetime. By becoming aware of the abuse, owning it, and recognizing the cycles, we can begin to wonder, "Why do people abuse" in the first place? Let's take a look in the next chapter.

PART TWO

Abuse Exhumed

Identifying Family Secrets

Chapter Three

Why Do People Abuse?

F amily photograph albums remind us of good times. However, it's the moments among the pages that often are the most memorable — often for the wrong reasons. A client, Cindy, brought in photos from her childhood that her mother had given her. Cindy was confused as to why some of the pictures bothered her so much. As I looked at them, it was clear from her expressions and body language that something was off with her and her brother. Upon further discussion, Cindy revealed that her brother had molested her from the ages of eight through fourteen. As we begin to identify the family secrets holding us back, and patterns we've naturally followed, I hope this chapter becomes one of the most eye-opening for you, as it was for Cindy.

As suggested, our genetic code has been handed down from many *generations*, but more recently from our grandparents. Additionally, their upbringing (or *conditioning*), traumas and abuse (*circumstances*) affected how they raised your parents, who also come hard-wired in certain ways unique to your family. Your parents grew up into an entirely different era from their folks' formative years, so they had to adapt to other stresses.

Then, we were raised in a completely different era, characterized by such things as new technologies and ease of travel. Our kids tend to be raised on mobile devices rather than on the farms or learning a trade like our great-grandparents.

There are a host of reasons why someone would become an abuser, even if they don't realize it or want to acknowledge it. In this chapter, I'll explain a variety of reasons to help understand the causes, and potential solutions.

To start off, one example comes from the Duluth Model, which blames society for teaching men to assert male dominance over women, with a motivation for "power and control." While the model has forged a strategy that involves several community organizations to support the rehabilitation of men, I believe the main precept is partially true to some batterers, but doesn't account for many other possible reasons.

Often, the abuser is not motivated by power and control, as the Duluth Model suggests. For some abusers, the behavior is more automatic and reactive, as is the response from the abused. It is as if they are playing out a scripted role written generations before. Here are a couple of examples:

When asked by her therapist, "Have you ever been abused?" Nicole said, "No." But then, for a split second, she looked downward and frowned. Instinctively, her therapist knew something was off. A few more minutes of probing revealed a boyfriend with anger problems. During fits of rage, he would destroy her personal property, grab her and not let her go, and call her obscene names. One time, he dragged her out of the car, then turned the car around to run her over. She dodged the car, and had to walk quite a distance before hitching a ride home from a stranger. Yet, Nicole still did not see his behavior as abusive.

In a different therapy session, Nate was asked the same question. His first answer was also "No," but when he was asked to describe his relationship with his brother, he said it was non-existent. Further inquiries revealed his parents would lock him and his older brother in a room to "figure it out" when arguments arose. That led to Nate being physically and verbally beat up as a child, called a "loser," a "weakling," and "always in the way." On one occasion, Nate was held underwater by his brother until he passed out and needed to be revived. Yet again, Nate did not see that behavior as abusive, but the impact hurt him in different ways. He struggled with emotional overeating and couldn't hold down a relationship, largely due to poor self-esteem, which became virtually non-existent.

For Nicole and Nate, abusive behavior became acceptable. While neither of them would tolerate a friend being abused in similar manners, it had become okay for them. Even after being confronted, they defended their abusers, took responsibility for their abuser's behavior, and minimized the impact.

Over time, therapy helped Nicole to gain the strength to tell others about what was happening, and stand up for herself. Nate also gained the strength to write a letter to his brother regarding the abuse, while gradually testing new boundaries with him. It worked, and today the brothers have a better relationship.

HOW DOES THIS HAPPEN?

I've categorized abuse patterns into three types:

1. **Generational:** Abuse learned, or passed down genetically, and from the family tree.
2. **Conditional:** How we were raised, including the environments, cultures, and behaviors that formed our belief systems and understanding of abuse and right and wrong.
3. **Circumstantial:** When generational and conditional patterns add up, various circumstances can apply pressure that forces the situation to escalate. If left without being addressed, the problem will likely repeat.

These are broad categories, but with them, you can ask yourself, "How does this apply to me?"

First, examine the possible generational factors hard-wired into your family history. Then, consider your upbringing and the various conditions that came into play in your development. Between these first two categories, you can already see how each one of us has certain vulnerabilities. When the triggering circumstance occurs, it's like the straw that breaks the camel's back.

13 REASONS WHY PEOPLE ABUSE

Hands down, the number-one question I get asked in therapy is "Why would they do this?" Mostly, this stems from a person who has been abused and is trying desperately to understand why their attacker is abusive. There are many forms of abuse, as we will see in coming chapters, but typically they fall into these basic categories: verbal, mental, emotional, physical, sexual, financial, and spiritual. Even if a person realizes the full scope of their abuse, it is difficult to comprehend why someone would do that to them.

Please note that I'm not intending to explain, justify, or rationalize abuse. Nor am I trying to elicit empathy or sympathy for the abuser. Abuse is wrong all the time, under all circumstances, regardless of the severity. Rather, the intent is to shed light on a question that plagues the abused, to gain understanding that all people do not have the same perspective of right and wrong, and to move the healing process further for those who have been damaged.

Here are thirteen reasons why a person becomes abusive:

1. **They were abused:** Some abusers act out their dysfunctional behavior on others because it was done to them. In a subconscious effort to resolve their own abuse, they do the same to another person. This type of abusive behavior is identical, meaning it almost exactly matches their childhood experience. Another example throws this past in the opposite direction. For instance, a boy who is sexually abused by a man might

grow up to sexually abuse girls as evidence that he is not a homosexual. The reverse can be true as well.

2. **They have a disorder:** A small fraction of the population has antisocial personality disorder (sociopathic or psychopathic) and is sadistic. People with these disorders gain pleasure from seeing others in pain and even more pleasure when they are the ones inflicting the agony. For them, abuse is a means to an end. They abuse others to gain personal pleasure, which follows the Duluth Model for explaining abuse as a method to assert power and/or control.

3. **They are addicted to alcohol and/or drugs:** Whether under the influence or not, the addicted person is not completely in control of his or her own thoughts, words, and behaviors. When under the influence, they can justify just about anything, including abusive behaviors. When sober, they are irritable, because their brain and body are waiting for the next fix. People who are associated with addicts often enable the addictions, becoming doormats or offering excuses for the addicts' choices, which are lies.

4. **They have seen or heard something hostile:** With the advances in technology comes additional exposure at a young age to glorified abuse. Some movies, songs, TV shows, and video games minimize abuse by making fun of it or making it seem normal. They may even give the abuser new ideas.

5. **They have anger issues:** Uncontrolled and unmanaged rage frequently produces abusive behavior. The source of this anger varies, but it is usually tied to a traumatic event or pattern. Unresolved trauma sparks anger when triggered by a person, circumstance, or place. Because this anger comes out of nowhere, it's that much harder to control and manifests abusively. This type of abuser is easier to spot, as the abuse is almost always preceded with an anger outburst. Many people

stay with this type of abuser believing that if they help to minimize the rage, everything will be different.

6. **They grew up with an addict:** An addict blames others for the reason they engage in their destructive behavior, while their victims are often forced to remain silent and acceptant of their behavior. The end result is a lot of pent-up anger and abusive behavior. As an adult, the victim subconsciously seeks out others to blame for their actions.

7. **They have control issues:** Some people like to be in charge, which is also a characteristic of the Duluth Model. In an effort to gain or remain in control of others, they utilize inefficient means of dominance, such as bullying or intimidation. While forced control can be executed quickly, it does not last. True leadership is void of abusive techniques.

8. **They don't understand boundaries:** Abusive people tend to lack the understanding of where they end and another person begins. They see their spouse/child/friend as an extension of themselves and therefore believe that other person is not entitled to have any boundaries. A lack of healthy boundaries opens the door for the power-hungry abuser.

9. **They are afraid:** People who do and say things out of fear tend to use their emotions as justification for why another person needs to do what is demanded. It is as if the fear is so important or powerful that nothing else matters except what is needed to subdue it. So, they abuse because of their fear, and because the abuse is their dysfunctional way of generating the same fear in others. Think: Misery loves company.

10. **They lack empathy:** It is far easier to abuse others when there is no empathy for how the victim might feel. Some types of head trauma, personality disorders, and environmental traumas can cause a person to lack the ability to express empathy. Without empathy, abuse is just a means to an end.

11. **They have a personality disorder:** Just because a person has a personality disorder, that does not mean that they will be abusive. However, after working with many people with personality disorders, I've seen how the disorder feeds into an inaccurate perception of reality, which increases the risk of abusive behavior. If a person is unable to see their behavior as abusive (a common trait for narcissists, psychopaths or sociopaths), then they will keep doing it.

12. **They are exhausted:** When a person reaches the end of their rope, it is not uncommon for them to lash out at whoever is conveniently close. Think of it as a mental breakdown where all the things stuffed inside come pouring out, usually in a destructive, rather than a constructive, manner.

13. **They are defensive:** Defense mechanisms such as denial, projection, regression, and suppression are utilized when a person is backed into a corner. Instead of taking space, they come out swinging and retaliate in an abusive manner, frequently in a passive-aggressive manner.

An abuser may have one, some, or all of these qualities, depending on the circumstances. There are many other possible reasons why one person might abuse another, but the predominant one is that they were abused at some point. While the intensity and type of abuse might vary, most abusers take their frustrations from their own abuse out on other victims. Because their abuser might not be present, might be an authority figure, or might still be a threat, they find new victims on whom to release their rage. This can be done at conscious and subconscious levels.

Knowing why someone abuses helps to round out the whole story. It doesn't excuse the abuse, but putting it in context can lead to understanding and, eventually, forgiveness.

WHEN REASONS ARE MYSTERIOUS

Sometimes, even for a licensed therapist, the reasons someone acts out in abusive ways can seem mysterious. Maybe they exhibit many of the reasons above, or none at all. Then one day, "Boom"! —something triggers unexplainable behavior.

One time, Sam, a client, came to me fearing for his life. His father had died "accidentally," but he suspected that his brother, who was living in the same house, may have murdered him. Sam said his brother was never violent and seemed to be a normally functioning adult, although struggling to make ends meet. Not too long after I met with Sam to help him with his fears, his brother broke into his house with a gun and shot him, then shot himself to death. Sam lived to tell the story. Upon further investigation, we learned that his brother had suffered head trauma (traumatic brain injury or TBI) along with a few strokes, which had negatively affected his brain.

We traced the brother's behavior and realized that we could pinpoint when he started taking a turn for the worse—right after he was "healing" from the strokes.

Sometimes, abuse is not a result of any of the reasons listed above. Instead, the true cause is biological—a result of a damaged brain, whether from alcohol or drug use, or a traumatic brain injury.

I learned a powerful lesson with Sam: If the reasons for abuse seem mysterious, or if we're stuck with the current therapeutic process and not seeing results, I highly recommend "opening the hood" and getting a brain scan—in Sam's case, it would have been for his brother. I refer clients to get a SPECT (single photon emission computed tomography) scan from one of the clinics of Dr. Daniel G. Amen, the renowned author, neuroscientist, and psychiatrist to help with the diagnosis.

The SPECT scan differs from other scans, because it shows "activity" in the brain, or blood flow, to identify where the brain is under- or overactive. This can reveal biological reasons for behaviors. For example, if the prefrontal cortex is damaged, that will explain impulsiveness, bad decision making and errant behaviors. Dr. Amen's work reviewing tens of thousands of brain scans, including the largest study ever done with professional football players, helps to reveal areas of the brain that may have suffered from previous traumatic brain injuries, among other insights that explain poor behavior.

In a groundbreaking study, named by *Discover Magazine* in 2015 as of the top twenty science stories of that year, Dr. Amen and other researchers used SPECT scans to distinguish between TBI and post-traumatic stress disorder (PTSD).[12] Prior to that time, TBI and PTSD could not always be positively identified. Moreover, treatments for TBI and PTSD are usually very different. If an accurate diagnosis isn't made, incorrect prescriptions or therapeutic methods could do more harm than good. But with a SPECT scan, the treatment can be more appropriate.

One client, who was a veteran of the Iraq war, brought home a Dr. Jekyll/Mr. Hyde-like condition. He would seem completely normal but then would disappear for days on an alcoholic binge and turn into a monster. His family didn't know what was going on, or what to do to help. We sent him in for a brain scan, and we found answers.

While serving our country in Iraq, my client, like thousands of war veterans, experienced incidents and injuries that civilians only see in movies. For this man, the brain scan revealed signs of TBI and PTSD. That helped me with a new line of questioning. We learned two things: First, the TBI was caused by a grenade blast, which knocked him out and took his hearing; second, he had to shoot and kill many people at close range. Unlike violent video games, the reality of war left an impression on his brain that could not be easily removed, especially if he continued drinking heavily. We were able to get him into an alcohol treatment facility, while we processed the war-time traumas that led to self-destructive behavior.

---

12. Amen, D.G., Raji, C.A., Willeumier, K., et al. Functional Neuroimaging Distinguishes Posttraumatic Stress Disorder from Traumatic Brain Injury in Focused and Large Community Datasets. *PLoS One*. 2015;10(7):e0129659. Published 2015 Jul. 1. doi:10.1371/journal.pone.0129659.

Another case involved a race car driver who came to see me. He had been abusing his wife, completely losing it with rage, throwing things, and he feared he would get physically abusive. He had always been "super chill," a nice guy with a great personality. He didn't have any personality disorder or history of abuse in the family. We couldn't figure out the underlying reasons for his scary behavior, so we suggested a brain scan for him.

We found a TBI and evidence of marijuana abuse. Sure enough, when we met again, I was able to focus on what the scans told me. He told me he had had several accidents while racing. Despite wearing a helmet, the brain is a soft organ that can be damaged when sloshed around abruptly. We added up about five concussions (a mild TBI), which were not able to heal properly, largely due to his preferred method of relaxing, smoking marijuana.

Concussions have a profound impact on the brain, especially if they are not given the time and attention to heal properly. They can be dangerous for everyone around, especially the one with the concussion. These TBIs can add up and create a degenerative condition known as "chronic traumatic encephalopathy" (CTE), which was made more famous from the movie *Concussion,* featuring actor Will Smith. If you haven't watched it, I highly recommend it.

Nowadays, I always ask clients about previous head trauma, but it's not that easy, because we aren't used to believing that a knock on the noggin could result in such bad behavior. It's hard to remember at times, but the SPECT scans show that the brain doesn't easily forget.

Now that we've covered some of the reasons, in the next chapter, I want to address the victims and abusers, with therapeutic suggestions. After all, knowing why abuse occurs is only half the battle, because the war for healing requires some strategy, too.

Chapter Four

For Victims and Abusers

With abuse, there are numerous sides to the story, each with a long line of generational, conditional, and circumstantial potential for the abuser and victim. As we further investigate family matters, I hope we don't get into a blame game. That's why I started with acknowledging that both the abuser and the victim often play a role. The more we take responsibility for our own safety and decisions, the easier it will be to heal from the past.

Unfortunately victims unintentionally attract abusive behavior by ignoring their intuition, believing everyone is kind, or suppressing past abuse. This may sound hard to believe, but often the abuser is a psychological mirror that the victim doesn't believe can change. But it can.

Victims often remain in abusive relationships of their own accord. Whether they realize it or not, the abuse begins a conditioning process that tweaks the normal paradigm of understanding about love, grace, and kindness—even arguing as mature adults. The victim assumes that the other person has the best intentions, and they ignore red flags of dangerous behavior. Victims will take on excessive responsibility, be quick to forgive, and live beneath a façade that everything is okay. That sets the stage for abuse to occur. Abusers actively seek out victims who will easily comply, won't say, "No," and are naïve and unaware of their surroundings and/or potential threats. For example, a potential victim might be an attractive woman who is drinking too much at a bar, alone late at night—even if she "knows better." An abuser sees this woman as potentially easy prey. She is intoxicated so her defenses are down, she is alone so no one will notice what is happening, and it is night so no one is likely to miss her until morning.

Most acts of abuse are not "surprise" attacks. Typically, the abuse has been brewing for a while, if not decades, with plenty of warning signs. To stop the abuse, the victim needs to exit the cycle. The victim and abuser should get professional counseling. Note that counseling is more effective when received individually. If they engage in counseling together, this sets up the victim to be abused even further in counseling. Unfortunately, abusers are sometimes very charming and can be intentionally misleading, even to therapists.

Then, after a substantial period of awareness, healing, and restitution, they may be able to enter into another relationship. My rule of thumb is that it takes six months to a year for real change to take lasting effect. So, relationships should be put on pause during this period of time. This allows for relapse, setbacks, new boundary setting, and rediscovery of a relationship without abuse.

From the moment we were conceived, we have been receiving instructions from our parents and their DNA about our future. Throughout our gestation, how well our mother and father cared for themselves prior to conception, handling stresses and immunity challenges, influences our brain's development. Even as infants, we were able to sense fear, rage, and pain, which continued the coding process for future abuse possibilities. From the ages of three through seven, our identity as well as our understanding of family units and how they work were established. We didn't have a choice in how we were raised, nor did our parents. So, it's futile to blame your parents. Instead, choose to look beyond your upbringing and instead raise your children according to new values and priorities. This is how we can improve the family unit and finally cut the abuse cord. Still, most of the time, abuse patterns are passed down from our family, and they need to be addressed.

That's why I want to start this chapter by addressing you. Before opening some doors to the past, or planning the future, let's start with the here and now—with you.

IF YOU ARE THE VICTIM

If you are being injured or stolen from, or if anything illegal is happening to you, please CALL THE POLICE or file a report online with your local police department. Record, photograph, or use video to prove the extent of the incident, physical injury, or other damage. The injuries may require you to see a doctor or even visit the emergency room for medical supervision. If calling the police is out of the question for now, activate an escape plan whereby you can be around safe people and, if necessary, in a secret spot. If you are out of options, contact Victim Connect (victimconnect.org) for guidance.

It is important to tell someone about your abuse, whether it's a friend, therapist, family member, or clergy. This is not a journey to go on alone.

By this point in the book, you may have already noted abuse experienced in your life. As suggested, I hope you can acknowledge the abuse and perhaps how you tolerated the treatment. But that doesn't make the abuse okay. Something needs to change before the situation gets worse. If your intuition is telling you there is a danger or that something is off in the relationship or situation, listen to it. If some of those warning signs listed above ring true with you, then it's time to stop. Think. If you are the abuser, you can stop. If you are the victim, you can get away. Make the changes. Move on. It could mean saving your life.

- How often do you feel threatened?
- When was the last time?
- Do you have bruises, scars, other marks on your body, hair that's been pulled out or have other signs of physical attacks?
- Do you have anywhere, toward anyone, to go to for an escape?
- Have you set aside money or credit cards to help with the escape?

I've broken down many other types of abuse, with questions directed at each one, in Part 3 of the book. But for now, if you are in physical and/or emotional danger, then your safety and security become your top priorities.

Maybe you're not in immediate danger, but abuse from your past or family may continue to have a grip on your life. Victims tend to hold on and suppress the memory, believing they are moving past it. But like any injury, physical or emotional, a scar tends to get left behind. When scratched, the abuse can get stirred up from your past and catch you by surprise. For me, that moment came after the rape memory was unboxed during a dinner conversation. It may look different for you, but you can do something about it. You have to. Why?

Ignoring the problem just delays the potential for abuse to you and others around you, including your children—even if you don't have any now. Dealing with this issue can retrain your brain, rewrite your story from a healthy perspective, and prevent abuse in the future.

Regardless of the causes, you may need professional counseling or therapy. Trying to move past this on your own will become fruitless quickly. You may even need to confront your abuser, perhaps with a specialist like me.

WHY OLD ABUSE IS TRIGGERED

A client, Anne, came to me complaining of anger outbursts, and "losing it" for almost no reason. What was triggering this pattern? Her daughter really enjoyed swimming and wanted to spend more and more time in the water preparing for her next meet. Little did Anne want to admit, her daughter's passion for swimming was triggering horrific memories. We dove into therapy and started unpacking Anne's experience having been sexually abused by her own swim coach. Anne had buried these thoughts for years, but they were coming back up in the form of rage as an adult. Growing up, Anne was also highly competitive, with Olympic aspirations. She spent a lot of time in the pool and with her coach, who was "grooming" her to feed his deviant behavior. Anne's coach would justify his behavior by saying, "If I do this with you, then I don't have to do this with the other girls." Anne thought she was protecting her teammates, but in fact, they were being abused, too.

Now, a mother to a daughter swimming down the same memory lane, Anne wanted to protect her. She had to release these emotional ties and allow her daughter to excel in the sport they both loved, without the threat of abuse by the coach.

How does this happen? One way a person learns to cope with intense trauma or abuse is to dissociate or detach from their immediate surroundings. For some, this is a natural reaction born out of a survival instinct. For others, it requires effort and practice to shut down feelings, intentionally ignore surroundings, and completely disengage. In the case of long-term abuse (whether it's physical, emotional, mental, verbal, financial, spiritual, or sexual), the dissociating can reoccur as a post-traumatic stress-like reaction when triggered by a similar situation, object, or person. In Anne's case, the trigger occurred when her daughter took an interest in competitive swimming.

What happens at the moment? This unexpected response activates feelings of anxiety, panic, or even paranoia as fear cripples the person into believing that they will never be free from the abuse. For those like Anne, who don't remember the event initially, it can come back like a flood. Even those who have learned new coping mechanisms, healed from the trauma, and done considerable therapy to recover can still be affected. This does not discount the work done previously; rather, it is a manifestation of reality and the intensity of the abuse. This is also called "complex post-traumatic stress disorder" (CPTSD).

Why is this happening? Most people don't realize the full impact of an abusive situation when they are in the middle of it. This is especially true when the abuse occurs as a child. Children have a unique ability to bury difficult situations, hide from harmful people or environments, and discount the hurt. As adults, this is far more problematic, because life experiences tend to build on each other, especially negative ones, resulting in the potential for a volcanic type of emotional response. Adults who hear about or witness children experiencing the same level of abuse usually react protectively as they simultaneously become aware of the severity of their mistreatment. This, in turn, brings the maltreatment to the surface with greater-than-expected emotional reactions.

What can be done? This is the ideal time to reach out for help from a professional who specializes in your kind of abuse, to help you heal from the abuse that occurred. Trying once again to bury the event and ignore the feelings will only increase the intensity of reaction and delay the recovery process. It usually spills out as anger toward those closest to the victim, which can create unnecessary dysfunction in an otherwise functional relationship. The process is not as time-consuming as most believe, but it is specific to each event.

What is involved with healing? Sometimes, even when healing has already occurred, a dissociative reaction can be triggered by a new situation or person. This does not invalidate the healing process; rather, this is a time to remind the person that they have recovered. By remembering the transformation from victim to victor and the lessons learned about self and others through recalling the progression, a person can experience further healing. The simple act of reminding a person where they began and where they now are helps to create a more realistic perception.

Why are the feelings more intense now? In many cases, a victimized person is so numb when the abuse occurs that they feel very little. When this is compared to a healed person who is more self-aware of their emotional responses, the feelings appear to be more intense than they really are. This is similar to watching a sporting event from the top of a stadium without assistance, in contrast to watching it with binoculars. The binoculars provide clearer vision, and everything seems more intense when it seems closer. Feelings work in the same manner. It is not always because a person has not healed properly from an event that they are hurting now. Instead, it can be because they are aware of their feelings, now that it hurts.

How can a proper perspective restore peace? When a more accurate perspective is brought to light, a person can quickly reduce anxiety and restore peace. It is also beneficial to speak words of encouragement, reminding the victim that the cycle of abuse can be broken. Being re-triggered by an event, object, or person does not mean a loss of freedom. Viewing these events as an indication of progress from the reality and intensity of the abuse is therapeutic.

By seeking out a therapist, Anne was finally able to heal from her traumatic abuse as a child. She reached out to her former swim teammates and discovered some of them, too, were suffering from their own abuse. So, they created a new team of support that helped each other and their families. That gave Anne a much better perspective and a greater awareness of victims and victors.

IF YOU ARE THE ABUSER

FOR YOUR OWN SAKE, get help before your family or someone else calls the police or takes other actions that will ruin your life, because eventually they might.

Maybe you picked up this book because you've been thinking about trying to change, or you just want to learn what is being advised to victims of abuse. Regardless of the reasons, I'm glad you landed here.

Wisdom is more valuable than learning, because wisdom requires a decision. My hope is that you are seeking wisdom, for your own good and the lives of those around you.

Believe me, you are not immune to the damage caused. It doesn't matter how much money you've accumulated or what influence or power you've attained. As soon as you are reported to the police and arrested for abuse, that little mugshot of yours might even go on the Internet, and anybody might be able find out about it, forever.

I've seen many people lose their jobs, their marriages, their children—basically everything—over one incident. I cannot stress that enough: One incident of abuse can result in you losing literally everything. That goes for domestic violence, child abuse, and sexual abuse for starters.

For marriages, it doesn't matter what state you're married in: if you have committed physical violence, your victim's attorney may go after you for everything you're worth. They can tie you up financially with multiple hearings and motions, and they can ensure that the public knows that you have perpetrated some type of physical, sexual, or other abuse.

Once the police are involved, there are certain jobs you will automatically lose, or never get, just because of an accusation. You don't need to be proven guilty or innocent to lose your job—you can lose a job for an accusation and police record. Today, many employers will ask whether you have committed any crimes of violence, or whether anyone has ever accused you of committing these crimes—the primary ones involving domestic violence or child abuse. To verify your words, it's common to run a criminal background check on job applicants, and these days they can cost less than $100. If an employer finds out about your past, or that you've lied on an application, then there's little chance of getting another job, regardless of where you go.

Here's another example: A nineteen-year-old young man had sex with a sixteen-year-old girl, thinking that it was okay because the girl consented to it. But guess what? Her parents didn't consent to it, and they filed the charges because in Florida, the age of consent is eighteen years old, so sexual intercourse with someone who is under eighteen can be considered statutory rape. Now the young man has a sexual assault record, which follows him everywhere. He can't live within a certain radius of a school or a playground. With every job he applies for, he has to disclose his predicament, or his past can be found out when the employer conducts a background check.

One incident can ruin your life, because it can stick with you forever.

A seventy-five-year-old man with severe health problems and an alcohol addiction came into counseling. He seemed so sweet and had a successful career, but he was plagued by what he had done when he was twenty. In session, he confessed to me about raping a young woman. He, too, had buried the incident, but now, toward the end of his life, he was being tortured by seeing her face in nearly every young woman he ran into. The mind is an interesting thing.

You don't want any of these examples to happen to you. So, before you get to the level where someone has to call the police, file a restraining order, or seek some other injunction against you, all of which can be found out through a public record, do yourself a big-time favor and get some help immediately. You can stop this pattern and get better before it destroys your life. I've included some ways you can start to make reparations below, but there's no formula for honest repentance.

There are therapists who specialize in working with various types of abusers (including sexual offenders) who are particularly experienced in this form of trauma. Don't waste your money on the first therapist you find. It's got to be somebody who works and understands your specific area of abuse.

If you're not a sexual offender, but you have otherwise physically abused someone, I suggest finding a counselor or therapist who works with abusers, and "batterers."

For the less-obvious forms of abuse, you may have to do a little more digging. Perhaps you've started to see some generational, or more likely conditional, factors that have led you to behave or say things that hurt others, even unintentionally. For example, my family has a long history of being very good and talented at guilt-tripping. I am no exception. My kids would point out that I would default to guilt-tripping if I didn't know what else to do. I had to learn how to own this fact and allow my kids the right to be able to correct me when I was doing it, and redirect the energy into explaining the true purpose of my point in the conversation. The more ways I can talk to my kids about real-life issues like this, the better.

> **GUILT-TRIPPING**—OFTEN a passive-aggressive or intimidating tactic to cause someone else to feel guilty for the purpose of manipulating their behavior (e.g., "If you don't do what I say, I'll tell Mom about what you did.").

Guilt-tripping is a common tactic that a lot of parents use to coerce their kids into doing something, even if it seems harmless. If we teach kids to do something out of guilt, then we open them up to other types of abuse from people who use guilt-tripping.

Every abuser, whether they perpetrate more obvious forms of abuse or more subtle forms, must learn through humility to recognize, take accountability, identify why, and apologize for their role, while allowing others to correct them. Below, I've outlined the steps you can take, as they have been tried and proven.

7 STEPS ABUSERS CAN TAKE WITH THEIR VICTIMS

After reviewing the types of abusive behavior on the checklist, a client of mine, Mariah, identified the abuse she had received as well as the abuse she had given. Her mother had been verbally, mentally, and physically abusive with her as a child, something that Mariah had pushed aside and had not confronted until in therapy. But what really saddened Mariah was her becoming aware of how she was passing down some of the same abusive behavior onto her husband and children.

She told herself that because she didn't hit her kids, she was not abusive. But she was, in different ways. Her kids endured timeouts that were unusually long for their age. The standard for child development is one minute for every year a child has been alive. The last time she disciplined her six-year-old, the child was sent to a dark closet for fifteen minutes when six minutes in her room would have been plenty.

She was also verbally abusive, calling her husband names in front of the kids and referring to her kids as "stupid." Mentally, she twisted the truth and was very manipulative with her husband, adding some emotional abuse by guilt-tripping him and the kids into doing things she wanted. In order to prevent her family from becoming aware of her lies, she would gaslight them and make them feel like they were going crazy.

As Mariah read through the checklist, she was overwhelmed by her behavior and vowed to be different. But there is an art to accepting responsibility in a way that demonstrates understanding of the mistake and sufficient remorse to not repeat it, and that gives empathetic treatment for the victim. Saying, "I'm sorry," would not be sufficient in this case. Mariah needed to do more.

1. **Acknowledge Internally.** The first step Mariah took was to admit precisely what she had done wrong, internally. This was not about blaming her mother or her childhood. This is the most critical step, because it is not about what others see; rather, it is a condition of the heart. Mariah needed to recognize that her abusive behavior was wrong and hurtful to others, and then choose to amend it. Many people fake this first step in order to look good in front of others or to blame others for their behavior, but without acknowledging the pain they have inflicted on others, no real positive change can occur.

2. **Confess to Another.** This step can be embarrassing and is often skipped for that reason. Mariah confessed her abusive behavior to her therapist first, to gain more insight and an accurate perception before talking to her family. When a person has

done wrong to a victim, confessing their behavior to another person allows there to be a level of accountability. Doing it before confronting the victim, allows the offender a greater understanding of the severity of the abusive behavior. The goal here is to stop or prevent passing abuse from one generation to the next. Mariah worked therapeutically through the abuse she had received and given, before confronting her family.

3. **Admit to the Victim.** Mariah began by talking to her husband first, and then they decided how and when to talk to the kids. There are two good ways to confess abuse to a victim: writing a letter/email or orally declaring it. Making general statements like "I'm sorry for all the hurt I caused you," however, is not sufficient. That is a way to dodge responsibility, because there is nothing specific to hold the person accountable. Rather, the statement should be, "I'm sorry for verbally assaulting you by calling you a name." By admitting her behavior to her kids, Mariah was also teaching her kids not to tolerate the same behavior in others.

4. **Declare Understanding.** During the confession, it is important to state how the offense hurt the victim. Mariah used her understanding of the impact of her abuse in that moment. For instance, to say, "You looked sad when I called you that name" accepts responsibility for a hurtful emotional response. Refusing to state that a painful remark caused unnecessary sadness opens the door for the abuse to be blamed on someone or something else. This step demonstrates a level of empathy for the victim that is essential to repairing the relationship.

5. **Erect a Boundary.** Mariah gave a lot of thought to what her boundaries should look like going forward. Saying, "If I do this again, I understand that you will . . . " demonstrates a grasp of the potential consequences for any further abuse. It is also a way of showing awareness for the severity of the offense. However, some people use this step as a way to

control the outcome or the consequences of future abuse. Taking the time to gather input from her husband and kids as to what the consequences should be gave them more control.

6. **Give Time.** After any offense/confession, the victim needs adequate time to believe the change is real. Mariah lost the right to state how long that time frame needs to be; rather, her husband and kids now have that control. Real change, like new habits, takes time to take hold in a person. Usually, several incidents of anger, anxiety, depression, or fear need to occur, before one can verify that the change is permanent. This process is not a straight line; rather, it is a crooked one that everyone concerned hopes is headed in the right direction.

7. **Be Accountable.** Mariah's husband, kids, and therapist all have the right to question her to see whether she is following through appropriately. A willingness to be accountable to other people for actions and behavior demonstrates maturity and responsibility. A break in this step indicates a person who has not truly changed.

Note that in all of the steps, nothing is required of the victim (in this example, Mariah's husband or kids). It is not the responsibility of the victim to do anything after having been offended. They can choose to forgive or not as they see fit. Instead, all of the steps focus on the actions, behavior, and attitude of the offender.

More often than not, we are both the abuser and the victim. Those who are neither an abuser nor a victim have a reason to learn more — perhaps for the sake of a family member. That's why it's important to learn about abuse from every angle.

FAMILY MATTERS

After reading this far, you've probably already identified some abuses you've never thought of before, and for reasons you never imagined. That's 100% okay. In fact, that's the purpose of this book — to help you identify how abuse has been prevalent in your life so you can make positive changes.

In the following chapters, we're going to break down different categories of abuse. As we look up your family tree, we can see that when it comes to abuse, family matters.

Here's an exercise that may be helpful. We call it a "genogram."

1. Draw a simple family tree, up through your grandparents' generation. For blended families, stick with your biological line the best you can.
2. On the left side, list any "generational," "conditional," or "circumstantial" examples of possible abuse that occurred with your grandparents, then with your parents. Include deaths and divorces as circumstances, for example.
3. On the right side, jot down any characteristics that you may have picked up.

I had a client, Brenda, who came to see me because she was an "absolute mess," crying all the time. That level of sadness surely points to depression, or does it? She had a great relationship with her husband and kids. She was a competent nurse, but she couldn't figure out why she felt so overwhelmed all the time.

We drew up her genogram, and Brenda was amazed at what we found. First, her mother had been unusually strict with her, saying, "You can't do this," or "You have to do that." It was always her way or the highway. But after examining Brenda's genogram, that was nothing compared to learning that her great-grandfather had killed his wife. Additionally, Brenda's grandfather had killed his first wife, burned his house down, and attempted to murder his second wife. He ended up dying in a weird accident later.

The story continued: Brenda's uncle was a convicted murderer, too. Virtually every male figure in Brenda's life had murdered his wife. Despite the gravity of it all, it was a beautiful thing to finally see in a tangible way that Brenda feared the worst. We found other seriously abusive people all over her family tree. We were able to sort this picture out and began to set healthy boundaries within Brenda's family. Now, Brenda is doing 10,000 times better.

It's amazing to see what is revealed when you see everything at once. Brenda's husband, a Christian pastor, was helpful in establishing boundaries. For example, he taught her that she could honor her mother from a distance. A funny thing happened: Once Brenda established that boundary, her mother lost control and would not reach out. Her mother no longer had Brenda for a whipping post. That's the reality of how little of a relationship had existed between them.

During this process, if any "family secrets" have come up, be careful with your next steps, whom to speak with, and how to integrate this new learning into your life moving forward. A new finding may be a shock and may explain a lot about the situation. Find a licensed therapist who specializes in your kind of case, and get help. It'll be the best investment of your life.

Chapter Five

Types of Abuse

This may be one of the most revealing chapters in the book. Abuse appears in various shapes and forms, but not all are easy to recognize. It's not always obvious, and sometimes the damage done does not rear its ugly head until later in life—in the form of PTSD or C-PTSD. Those might not always occur, but trauma and/or abuse left suppressed will come up again at the least-expected moments.

For example, one of the easiest ways to identify unrecognized trauma is an uncharacteristic anger outburst about something petty, or at least disproportionate to the reaction.

For example, one day, I was driving on a major highway, and there was a left-turn exit coming in the next half mile. I saw a glimpse of a motorcyclist without a helmet, and he was closing distance on me rapidly. He seemed to fly by my right side at least twenty miles per hour faster than I was going. Then he cut me off to make the left-turn exit. I slammed on my breaks, but if I hadn't seen him I would have killed him, quite frankly.

I was fuming mad. I was so worked up inside that I kept debating the issue in my head. I tried accepting the anger by saying to myself,

There is nothing wrong with how I am feeling right now, but that didn't work. It could have been a bad accident. But it wasn't. I was paying attention. Nothing happened to him, nothing happened to me. Why couldn't I let this go?

At that very moment, I asked myself a second question: *What does this remind me of?*

As soon as I thought those words, it automatically flashed before me: One of my closest friends from high school had been killed in a motorcycle crash. He had been making a left turn, and an oncoming driver had not seen him before crashing into his bike. My friend died instantly.

After recalling that, I realized that I was still angry about the incident and losing my friend. I needed to process his death fully and accept his fate. Within a few minutes, I was able to calm down from what had happened with me and the motorcycle driver.

In other cases, the abused will carry their pain over into the next conversation. For example, I could have carried my anger with me into my next appointment, but that would have tainted the entire session.

You may lose it at the cashier, or worse, lose your cool with your kids for acting like children regarding the dumbest things that don't even matter.

When you notice intense or unexpected anger, it might be a sign of unresolved trauma. Fear is sometimes responsible for the anger, as anger is easier to release than fear. Trauma and abuse instill fear into their victims, who can also be triggered by other seemingly less-critical indications. Anyone who has been physically or sexually abused carries a fear that it will happen again. That can cause hyper-vigilance, over-reaction, and emotional outbursts in situations that don't warrant the response. Fear and anger are base emotions that can be difficult to manage. Likewise, the desire to withdraw, drink excessively, use drugs, or abuse others is often an attempt to silence the uncomfortable emotions. When you identify trauma and abuse to be underlying anger and fear, you can see even more clearly the events that need healing.

ABUSE CHECKLISTS

Over the next few pages, I'll offer various checklists with explanations of the abuse. In this section, review the various examples and check off the ones that apply to you. If you have something to add, feel free to do so, because I cannot cover all the examples that may apply to you. Still, I've seen and treated a lot of examples, and they typically fall into these categories (in alphabetical order):

1. **Cyber Abuse**: Intimidation, threats, insults, and covert operations, often with falsified identities.
2. **Emotional Abuse**: Intense anxiety, guilt, confusion, shame, anger, hostility, rejection, and fear.
3. **Financial Abuse**: Sole control of money, stealing, destroying assets, hiding resources, refusing access, falsifying records, and interfering with work environments.
4. **Legal Abuse**: Using the legal system to tie you up in court unnecessarily.
5. **Medical Abuse**: Deciding about or preventing medical treatment. Illegal substances and pharmaceutical drugs are sometimes given without knowledge or consent.
6. **Mental Abuse**: Gaslighting, silence, manipulation, and victimization.
7. **Physical Abuse**: Intimidation, isolation, restraint, aggression, and endangerment.
8. **Self-Abuse**: Cutting, other self-harm, suicide attempts, picking, eating disorders designed to inflict pain on yourself to relieve emotional pain.
9. **Sexual Abuse**: Jealous rages, coercion, sexual withdrawal, rape, and degrading acts.
10. **Spiritual Abuse**: Dichotomous thinking, prejudice, elitist beliefs, excommunication, estrangement, and demanding submission.
11. **Substance Abuse**: Substance abuse can impact the family both directly and indirectly. Neither has good results.

12. Verbal Abuse: Screaming, bullying, name-calling, berating, and blaming.

Now it's your turn. Review the sections in the next chapter that offer checklists for each of these types of abuse. Check the ones that most relate to you. By no means is this an exhaustive list, so we've added extra space so you can fill in any examples from your life that are not listed already. Take your time reviewing the checklists. It is not uncommon to have flashbacks, anxiety, panic attacks, deep sadness, and/or intense anger as you look at the lists. Listen to your body, and take breaks, but do finish the lists. Remember: You can't heal from abuse if you don't first acknowledge it.

Checklist: Cyber Abuse

These days, all kinds of abuse can come right through the device in our hands. The mobile and computer age has spawned a whole new category of abuse, with terms like "cyberbullying," "cyberstalking," "catfishing," "spoofing," "flamebaiting," and "identity theft," along with other potentially dangerous harassment. That's why this checklist looks a little different, too. Cyber abuse is so covert, it's designed to be virtually impossible to detect—until it's too late. So, I've extended this section with explanations, while admitting that there are more cyber terms and abuse examples than I can address in writing. But this should help:

- ☐ **When Text Messages Turn Abusive**
  - ☐ **Love bombs.** Grooming often includes drawing in the victim with exciting, irresistible messages.
  - ☐ **Claims to have "never received" a text or "never said that."** Forms of gaslighting manipulation intended to make the victim think they are losing their mind—when evidence shows the contrary.

☐ **Refusing to answer.** Avoiding texts, refusing to answer certain questions, or sending confusing emojis are abusive tactics that lead to more manipulation and lies.

☐ **Over-texting.** Sending multiple messages to badger, interrupt, and demand immediate response (control). It includes sending excessively long text messages.

☐ **Sending unsolicited photos, messages.** Sending unwanted nude photos and "sexting" are tactics to see whom an abuser can hook. Such activities also include sending threats or false accusations and sharing "fake" news and/or images that threaten self-harm in order to get a response.

☐ **Inappropriate sarcasm, followed by "You can't take a joke."** Sarcasm does not always translate properly in text messages, because while the words can be humorous, they can also be devious, cutting, or serious. Accusing the reader of not being able to take a joke points the finger in the wrong direction. Abusers rarely want to talk through any confusion over the phone, because they don't care to listen.

☐ **Rush to meet in person.** Many abusers will plead to meet in person as soon as possible. By using text messaging, location and timing can be set up easily, often including an incentive to meet right away.

☐ **Cyber Trolling**—Viewing online profiles with an abusive intent is called "trolling." For example, before hiring you, a "troll" in the potential employer's office may try to find something in your online past that they can use against you. Sexual abusers also troll online, enticing victims too quickly with too much. This includes posting false identities on dating sites with the purpose of luring in victims.

☐ **Cyberbullying**—Bullying is an abusive tactic, and when "cyber" goes in front, it can become exponentially more harmful. Today's youth often face cyberbullying when (typically shameful) photos, videos or recordings are shared online without their consent, altered to fit the scheme, or used out of context to hurt, intimidate, or embarrass. If the material is not removed, it may stay online for years (until Google's parameters render it not "relevant"). The more times it is viewed, the more "relevant" it becomes, which extends its online lifespan.

☐ Often includes offensive name-calling, repetitive, and/or belligerent messages which are difficult to defend (e.g., "You're an idiot," "You'll never succeed," "Nobody cares about you," "I'd like to see you go down in flames.").

☐ **Cyberstalking**—Similar to cyber trolling, this practice focuses on an individual often crossing personal boundaries. **Note:** *Cyber Stalking is illegal in many states*, but it can be difficult to prove. There four main types:

☐ *Vindictive*: Cruel attacks intended to cause pain.

☐ *Composed*: The motive is to annoy and irritate the victim.

☐ *Intimate*: Attempts to form an intimate or abusive relationship.

☐ *Collective*: Groups formed with the purpose of taking down a person or organization.

Cyberstalking: Examples

☐ **False identities:** Stalkers will often set up anonymous or fake websites or blogs to post false information, false accusations, or false news.

☐ **Gathering information:** Scouring the Internet for personal information is often followed by the abuser approaching the unsuspecting victim's friends, family, and co-workers for details, which often leads to physical stalking, as the abuser begins to appear at the victim's locations. The practice includes using intrusive phone calls or wire-tapping, covert surveillance video, trespassing, vandalism, theft, and various forms of assault.

☐ **Monitoring:** The abuser uses the victim's online activity to monitor locations, friends, and favorite spots. This includes obtaining access to the victim's IP address and passwords to watch from a distance that's too close for comfort.

☐ **Flying monkeys:** Like the wicked witch from the famous movie, abusers sometimes recruit others to do their dirty work, asking them to harass the victim through online means.

☐ **Playing the victim:** Stalkers will turn the tables by making false claims about being harassed online by the victim.

☐ **Sending viruses:** Stalkers will manipulatively send computer viruses that only they can solve, in order to come across as having the ability to solve the problem or empathize with the victim, or just to ruin their lives.

☐ **Ordering products:** Stalkers will order or subscribe to embarrassing items using the victim's name, sometimes shipping the items to their workplace.

☐ **Spoofing:** The abuser pretends to be someone else, like a bank representative or other authority, to "verify" (obtain) personal information.

☐ **Online/Email Scams.** Stalkers will use various scams to obtain more information. Too-good-to-be-true offers received via email may be loaded with encrypted information to help the stalker.

☐ **Catfishing.** The perpetrator poses as someone else and creates a false social media identity. The name, photos, locations, and basic information can all be false. Sometimes, the perpetrator poses as the victim with the intention of fooling others and humiliating the real victim.

☐ **Flaming.** This tactic involves posting insults (usually laced with aggression or profanity) to incite the victim. The purpose is to draw the victim into a discussion or to fuel discourse between the perpetrator and the victim. **Flamebait** is a post that sparks anger or an argument.

☐ **Identity Theft.** After trolling and stalking, the abuser might have gathered enough personal information to steal the victim's identity. Abusers use this information to apply for credit cards and mortgages and to make purchases without detection.

☐ **Account Takeover.** Many people save passwords for their financial information on their electronic devices. A perpetrator can gain access to a victim's device, log onto the accounts, change passwords or addresses, send embarrassing emails, delete documents, and/or destroy the victim's reputation.

☐ **Other:** _____

_____

Checklist: Emotional Abuse

☐ **Nitpicking:** Whatever is important to you is minimized in comparison to the abuser's agenda. They belittle your accomplishments, aspirations, or personality in front of others. Teasing and/or sarcasm are commonly used to degrade and mock.

☐ **Embarrassment/Shame:** The abuser shares private information without consent, treats you like a child, or exposes some shameful event. They remind you of your shortcomings, often in a passive-aggressive way that is not in an overt manner, but hidden, and when least expecting it.

☐ **Increased Anxiety:** It is easy to become anxious when questioned about every move, motive, or aptitude. You feel overwhelmed from the excessive responsibility the abuser dumps on you. They also expect you to drop everything to "cheer them up."

☐ **Excessive Guilt:** The abuser claims that they should be the most important person in your life, and that it is selfish for you to take care of yourself.

☐ **Insecurity:** You are held to an unrealistic, unattainable, or unsustainable standard. Then when you fail, the abuser treats you as inferior.

☐ **Confusion:** Being treated as an extension of the abuser, not a separate person.

☐ **Alienation:** Belittling friends and family and making your social engagements a nightmare. (By contrast, they will be amazingly charming at their own social engagements).

☐ **Anger/Fear:** The abuser generates an angry response by acting immature and selfish but then accuses *you* of behaving that way. They may use intimidation, threats, frightening behavior, and/or destruction of treasured possessions.

☐ **Hostility:** Abusers may oppose the victim's thoughts, wants or concerns in unfriendly manners. This ongoing bitterness can become scary and make the victim feel like they can never do, say or think anything right.

☐ **Rejection:** An abuser may also refuse to acknowledge worth by withholding love or intimacy, creating a threat of, or obvious rejection.

☐ **Other:** _____

_____

Checklist: Financial Abuse

☐ **Forbidden Access:** Highly controlled access to money (e.g., accounts) or possessions to create a dependency on the abuser for food, clothing, shelter, and necessities. The abuser might maintain secret accounts at various financial institutions or deplete accounts without the victim's knowledge.

☐ **Unreasonable Allowances/Budget:** Treating spouses and children with an unreasonable allowance or budget demonstrates a controlling abuser who manipulates the victim into thinking they cannot be trusted or are not worth it. An abuser may put the victim on a strict allowance with an impossible "budget," thereby setting them up for failure. They may "punish" the victim for spending, with verbal, physical, sexual, or emotional abuse.

☐ **Theft/Fraud Exploitation:** An abuser may steal from, defraud, or exploit a victim and expect them to be okay with it. This includes being overly frugal and refusing to pay for necessities, as well as canceling or cashing out life insurance policies.

☐ **Assets:** An abuser may demand that all the victim's financial gifts, assets, or inheritances be placed in abuser's name. They may open bank accounts in their name without giving access to records, and they may cancel life, health, car, or homeowners insurance without your prior knowledge.

☐ **Paychecks:** An abuser may force your paychecks to be handed over and deposited in their account. They may also lie about their own income and how much is actually coming in.

☐ **Bills/Credit:** An abuser may put all the bills or credit cards in your name. They may want to keep any assets in their name, but any debt in your name. They may max out credit cards without your knowledge and ruin your credit rating.

☐ **Taxes:** An abuser may falsify tax returns to show inappropriate deductions and expect you to sign documents without question.

☐ **Career:** An abuser may forbid you from earning money, attending school, or advancing in a career.

☐ **Work:** An abuser may interfere in a work environment by calling your boss. They may insist on having access to your work emails and calendar so they can know details about your job. That is excessive and unprofessional and likely violates confidentiality. They may also harass or distract you at work through unannounced visits, excessive phone calls, or texting to negatively impact your job performance.

☐ **Other:** _____

_____

Checklist: Legal Abuse

☐ **Frivolous Lawsuits:** An abuser may make unnecessary court filings to try to impair your business and/or assets.

☐ **False Accusations:** False accusations put the opponent on the defensive with misinformation, causing the court to frown upon retaliatory accusations.

☐ **Entrapment:** An abuser may provoke irrational behavior followed by calling (or threatening to call) the police.

☐ **Gaming the System:** An abuser may use laws designed to protect a person as a way to manipulate the people in the situation. This is common in child custody cases.

☐ **Choosing Litigation Over Settlement:** Litigation costs can cripple an opponent, when a settlement could have been reached.

☐ **Tampering, Perjury, Other Illegal Tactics:** These acts may include falsifying filings to obtain restraining orders.

☐ **Other:** _____

_____

Checklist: Medical Abuse

☐ **Denying Medical Treatment:** Refusing to pay for, obstructing, or withholding, healthcare, and using rationales like "You're not really sick" or "You don't need a doctor for that" or alleging that the illness isn't real, but "just a figment of their imagination."

☐ **Deception About Medication:** This can range from giving placebos to overmedicating, as well as stealing or abusing the patient's prescription drugs. Watch out for parents or siblings who steal medication meant for treating attention deficit disorder (ADD), for example.

☐ **Maltreatment or Abandonment:** Providing incorrect medications, allowing self-medicating with alcohol, and refusing to follow the doctor's orders can all leave the victim vulnerable to many adverse side effects.

☐ **Gaslighting Medical Information**: An abuser may give false information to the victim, family, and/or caretakers so they are led to believe something other than the truth, and that they are losing their memories.

☐ **Lying to Physicians:** An abuser may go behind the back of the patient, and they may discount, minimize or lie to the doctor about the patient's problem. They may disingenuously insist that the patient is going crazy. They may plead to hospitalize the patient by falsely claiming suicide threats.

☐ **Exposing Medical Information:** An abuser might threaten to expose private medical information to others in violation of HIPAA laws. HIPAA, the Health Insurance Portability and Accountability Act, is a federal law designed to protect patient health information from being disclosed without the patient's consent or knowledge.

☐ **Other:** _____

_____

Checklist: Mental Abuse

☐ **Rage:** An intense, furious anger may come out of nowhere — usually over nothing significant — startling and shocking the other person(s) into compliance or silence.

☐ **The Stare:** An intense stare, with no clear feeling behind, it is frequently mixed with the silent treatment.

☐ **Silent Treatment:** Many abusers punish by ignoring. They may also have a history of permanently cutting others out of their life over small things.

☐ **Projection:** The abuser dumps their issues onto you as if you were responsible.

☐ **Twisting:** When confronted, the abuser will twist things around to blame you for their actions. They will not accept responsibility for their behavior and instead will insist on an apology from you.

☐ **Manipulation:** The abuser may engage in threats to make your worst fear come true, such as abandonment, infidelity, or rejection.

☐ **Victim Card:** When all else fails, the abuser may resort to playing the victim card to gain sympathy and further control your behavior.

☐ **Gaslighting:** This is a form of manipulation and psychological abuse by which an abuser makes the victim question their memory, perception, and sanity. The abuser denies, lies, or manipulates the facts about past behavior, thus further causing doubt about the truth. The gaslighter uses this method to change the victim's perception to gain something they want, like power or control or for the victim to be dependent on them.

Gaslighting has become a hot button recently. I'm finding that clients are often second-guessing themselves, excusing abusive behavior, and feeling as though they can't do anything right. The term derives from a 1938 stage play, *Gas Light*, which was later turned into a movie starring Ingrid Bergman as the victim of her husband's behavior. The movie includes an example in which the husband would slowly dim the gas lights in their home, while acting as if the lighting had not changed. His wife, the victim, would begin to doubt her own perceptions.

This tactic is common among sociopaths and narcissists. Gaslighters will flatly deny or even justify being physically abusive by distorting the truth so they falsely seem to preserve their "need to be right" in order to maintain power over their victim.

Saying, "You're crazy" or "Don't be paranoid" or feigning concern with "I'm worried about you because you don't seem well," are examples of the many other ways that gaslighting can result in a nervous breakdown or an inability to determine truth from fiction and right from wrong.

☐ **Other:** _____

_____

Checklist: Physical Abuse

☐ **Intimidation:** Bullying by standing over you, condescending, or getting "in your face" and then refusing to back off.

☐ **Isolation:** Limiting your ability to escape, or abandoning you in dangerous situations.

☐ **Restraint:** Confinement by blocking a doorway, grabbing you when trying to leave, locking doors with no key, tying you up, or depriving you of sleep.

☐ **Aggression:** Hitting, grabbing forcefully, kicking, punching, arm-twisting, pushing, beating, shoving, biting, slapping, striking with an object, shaking, pinching, choking, hair-pulling, dragging, burning, cutting, stabbing, strangling, and force-feeding (including overdosing or misusing drugs).

☐ **Endangerment:** Threats of killing, mixed with physical violence and use of weapons.

☐ **Other:** _____

_____

Notice that physical abuse goes beyond beating. It involves ways to utilize physical forces to win an advantage. Another unfortunate example is sleep deprivation.

Sleep Deprivation

One overt example of abuse focuses on the sleep cycle. A client of mine, Ralph, woke up in the middle of the night with a pillow covering his mouth and nose. He was laying on his back, and his wife had placed her pillow evenly on top of his head while her body straddled his. Instead of moving, he lay there silently, wondering how long she would keep the pillow there. As his breathing became more labored while she didn't move, he suddenly lifted his head and torso, startling her.

"What are you doing?" he asked, gasping for air.

"Nothing," she replied, "I was just joking."

But this was no joke. She was a registered emergency room nurse who understood the consequences of her actions. Added to that, the couple had been having significant marital problems. The rest of the night, Ralph lay in the bed listening in fear for any indicators that she would resume the suffocation attempt.

When Ralph brought up this incident in counseling, the therapist suggested that he press charges. He did not. He insisted that her behavior was not unusual, that she frequently disturbed his sleep.

This explained a lot of Ralph's peculiar behavior. He had trouble remembering details accurately, suffered from brain fog, lost things, had difficulty concentrating and controlling his emotions, and was unable to think clearly. He was sleep-deprived. As a subtle form of abuse, his wife was attempting to drive him crazy by depriving him of sleep. Here are some of her tactics.

1. **Waking him up after he fell asleep.** Ralph's wife would wake him up a couple of hours after he went to bed to rehash a disagreement from earlier in the day. She would claim that she was unable to sleep and needed to have a resolution, but there was none unless he agreed fully with her. When he did, she would belittle him by saying that he was just placating her so he could "get his precious beauty sleep."

2. **Claiming that he was snoring.** On a typical night, Ralph would be woken up by his wife at least twice with her complaining that he was snoring. One night, he recorded his sleep only to find out that he had not been snoring.

3. **Sharing paranoid thoughts and feelings just before bed.** Another tactic Ralph's wife used was stringing a random grouping of events together and drawing conclusions about him lying or cheating right before bed. This type of behavior caused Ralph to not sleep well as he struggled to understand her conclusions. Regardless of what he said, she was rarely satisfied.

4. **Punishment for napping.** After a week of poor sleep, Ralph would use the weekends to catch up on some of his sleep by

taking a nap. Instead of allowing him the needed rest, his wife would play loud music to try to wake him up. When he did get up, she would give him the silent treatment for ignoring her by taking a nap.

5. **Expecting him to video chat at night.** Because Ralph's wife sometimes worked the night shift at the hospital, she would require him to video chat with her just before going to bed. She insisted that he walk all around the house and show that no one was there, and then put his phone on her pillow. When he would fall asleep, she would wake him up by yelling.

6. **Inciting fear in the middle of the night.** Several times, Ralph was woken up in the middle of the night because his wife swore that she heard a strange sound in the house. She would not let it go until he got up out of bed to investigate the house. Then he was met with a barrage of questions about what he did and did not check.

7. **Making violent threats just before bed.** "I could kill you in your sleep, and no one would know," Ralph's wife would tell him. Before the suffocation threat, he took her comments with a grain of salt, but afterward, he was unable to sleep. He even moved to a spare bedroom, but that still did not help him sleep any better. He felt like he was sleeping with one eye open all night.

8. **Throwing water on him in the morning.** Exhausted from poor sleep the night before, when Ralph could, he would try to sleep in for a few extra hours in the morning. But if his wife were already awake, she would angrily throw cold water on him while he was in bed to wake him up from sleeping. She would then yell at him about being lazy.

9. **Attempting to have sex with him.** One of the stranger things Ralph experienced was his wife attempting to rape him while he was asleep. There were times when he woke up to find her body on top of his. When they were a newlywed couple, that

was exciting to him, but later he realized that the only times she wanted sex was when he was asleep.

These nine tactics caused Ralph to think he was losing it. He was not. He was just severely sleep-deprived. When he moved into an apartment without his wife, he was finally able to sleep. That restored his ability to make better decisions as he eventually saw his wife's behavior as abusive and sought a divorce.

While sleep deprivation is especially covert, narcissists may take this a step further. Here are at least five ways in which narcissists use physical abuse to rule over spouses.

5 Ways Narcissists Physically Abuse Spouses

Narcissistic spouses will blame others for their abusive behavior, instead of taking honest responsibility. "You made me upset," "If you won't say this (or act that way), then I won't have to get so forceful," or "It is because of you that I'm like this" are all typical remarks. Usually, these statements are sandwiched between half-hearted apologies (if you're lucky enough to get any at all).

There are many forms of physical abuse. Just because a mark was not left on a body, that does not mean that there wasn't cruelty, violence, neglect, and/or exploitation. Here is the progression of physical abuse:

1. **Intimidation:** The narcissistic spouse bullies their prey by physically looking down at them or getting "in their face" and then refusing to back off. They may even throw things, break things, or punch walls and doors that are dangerously close by. Even if there is no actual bodily harm, this intimidation feels actualized.

2. **Isolation:** The narcissist substantially limits their spouse's ability to escape, especially in dangerous situations. For instance, they might drive recklessly with no possible escape from the car. They might expose others to severe weather or environmental conditions. They might strand their spouse in

remote locations. All of this is done to force the spouse to rely solely on them and trust only their judgment.

3. **Restraint:** Physical contact begins in the form of holding a person back. The narcissist will confine their spouse by blocking a doorway, grabbing them when they try to leave, locking doors with no key, or tying them up. These actions cause a feeling (or reality) of false imprisonment, which is a warning sign to get out as immediately as possible. The next two steps are not that far behind.

4. **Aggression:** Remember, any physical force that results in pain, discomfort, or injury is completely unacceptable in any relationship. There are many types of aggression as listed in the checklist. Listen to your instincts, and if it feels aggressive, it *is* aggressive.

5. **Endangerment:** This is the most dangerous stage, because your life is in jeopardy. The intimidation, isolation, and/or physical or sexual abuse becomes so familiar you are now numb to the effects. Restraint becomes a waiting game that the victim and abuser master. Aggression is expected and is no longer shocking. The narcissist will realize that they are no longer commanding the same level of fear, so they escalate the attacks. If this feels familiar, do not stay—get out immediately.

Not all narcissists resort to physical abuse, and some never escalate beyond intimidation. Not all physical abusers are narcissists, and some have other mental illnesses. But a narcissistic physical abuser is not someone to take lightly. No matter what they say, you cannot make them better. That is a decision they need to make for themselves, and a process they must initiate and undertake, ideally away from you.

Checklist: Self-Abuse

(This type of abuse is self-induced,
while other types of abuse require another person.)

☐ **Self-Harm:** Dealing with pain is often expressed in unfortunate ways, including cutting, biting, picking, burning, pulling hair out, eating disorders (e.g., super-restrictive diets, overeating, and binging/purging), and alcohol/drug abuse.

☐ **Withdrawal:** Some avoid or refuse to get help when they know they need it, and some lie to friends and family members who confront them about self-harming behavior they can see (or see signs of).

☐ **Fear-Based Living:** Anxiety based on circumstances can lead people to isolate, refusing to leave the house or living in paranoia, agoraphobia, and other social anxiety. Each of these can lead to severe depression.

☐ **Sabotaging Self-Esteem:** Belittling yourself, believing that shame is a personal trait, obeying negative thinking, and poor hygiene indicate someone who is self-abusing.

☐ **Extreme OCD** (obsessive-compulsive disorder)**:** OCD behaviors and patterns become so intense that they cause you to miss social or family gatherings, perform poorly at work, hoard, or instate strict cleaning routines that everyone else is expected to follow.

☐ **Other:** _____

_____

Checklist: Sexual Abuse

☐ **Grooming:** The abuser may initiate an unwanted or embarrassing sexual act designed to catch you off-guard, create a feeling of trepidation, and see whether you comply.

☐ **Sexual Harassment:** The abuser threatens loss of income, job security, reputation, or promotion if the victim doesn't succumb to sexual advances. The unwanted advances and consequences might be direct, perceived, passive-aggressive, or covert.

☐ **Jealousy Rages:** An abuser may demand to be told everything about your previous sexual partners. Then they may use the information to call you promiscuous. They may make frequent accusations of your attraction to others, flirting, flaunting your body, and cheating.

☐ **Coercion Tactics:** Some abusers use harassment, guilt, shame, blame, or rage to coerce someone into having sex. They may nag, insult, become disruptive, or refuse to allow the other to sleep until they concede.

☐ **Threats of Infidelity:** An abuser may dangle the possibility of getting involved with another person in order to bully you into performing uncomfortable sexual acts.

☐ **Inciting Fear:** You could be expected to submit to unwanted sexual acts out of fear that you would be hit, left, humiliated, punished, or betrayed, or that money would be withheld.

☐ **Selfish Appeals:** One classic example of selfish sex is unprotected sex. Because abusive intercourse is all about how the abuser feels, they might refuse to use condoms and insist that you take full responsibility for birth control or STI protection.

☐ **Sexual Withdrawal:** Some abusers completely withdraw all sex from the relationship for no apparent reason. Any requests for sex are then met with ridicule, rants about performance, and excessive excuses for abstinence.

☐ **Ultimatums:** For the abuser, your body is theirs, and their body is theirs. Ultimatums include demands to lose weight or groom a certain way, forced pregnancy or an abortion, and forbidding breastfeeding.

☐ **Destroying Principles:** Your previous sexual standards are obliterated. For instance, participating in pornography or prostitution, having multiple partners at one time, or sex with animals were completely out of the question but might now be common.

- ☐ **Rape:** The FBI defines rape as "Penetration, no matter how slight, of the vagina or anus with any body part or object, or oral penetration by a sex organ of another person, without the consent of the victim."
- ☐ **Degrading Acts:** Degradation is in the eye of the beholder. The abuser might not view these acts as degrading, but you might. Here are a couple of examples: urinating on a person, having sex while on the toilet, or forcing sex in public places.
- ☐ **Sadistic Sex:** There are two forms of sadistic sexual acts: moderate (also known as "S&M") and severe, which can lead to death. Moderate examples include master-slave role-playing, immobilizing you through drugs or alcohol, administering pain (whipping) during sex, confining you to a cage, typing up, blindfolding, or clamping sexual organs. Severe examples include physical beatings, choking, psychological torture, burning, cutting, stabbing, vampirism, and murder before, during, or after sex.
- ☐ **Other:** _____

_____

Many times, the victim of sexual abuse fails to see the short- and long-term consequences in their life. It starts with shock. While the experienced sexual abuser plots out a plan and target, the victim is unaware. When the "surprise attack" occurs, the victim often says something like, "it happened so fast that I didn't have time or know what to do."

Victims who are lucky enough to escape their abusers may become disoriented or feel disgusted, violated, and/or frightened, so they do the first thing that comes to mind: Wash up to feel clean. That may erase the evidence, and it is an emotional way to respond to the crime and their feelings of desperation. That is why victims often have a difficult time assessing an abusive situation or knowing what to do next.

Unfortunately, if the victim withdraws and does nothing, the pattern of abuse will only be the beginning. They may fall prey to another abuser and say nothing. Or the victim may have to deal with others who call them names like "slut" and pick apart every tiny decision that led to the abuse, ultimately blaming them. These insensitive and ignorant remarks can re-traumatize the victim again.

This is why many victims of sexual abuse often choose silence and try to bury the burdens of guilt and shame. But the brain and body cannot forget, so these suppressed memories and feelings become emotional scars etched into their lives forever. Without forgiveness, safe boundaries, and processing the abuse with a therapist, triggers may open these wounds as if they had happened yesterday.

I hope to silence the ignorance of judgmental comments by others, and replace those with safe people who know that the number-one priority is the health and safety of the victim—not to belittle, disregard, or blame them. Sexual abuse crosses an intimate barrier that may also prevent the victim from having a healthy relationship in the future. However, time, therapy, and surrounding oneself with safe people are some keys to healing.

Checklist: Spiritual Abuse

☐ **Dichotomous Thinking:** The abuser may divide people into two categories: Those who agree with them and those who don't. They make fun of, belittle, and show prejudice toward others' beliefs.

☐ **Elitism:** Some people refuse to associate with people or groups they consider impure or unholy.

☐ **Submission:** This requires that you completely adopt their point of view. There is no room for differing opinions or questioning their authority. Name-calling, chastising, and the silent treatment are common maneuvers to impose compliance.

☐ **Labeling:** Others who don't comply with their beliefs are seen as disobedient, rebellious, lacking faith, demons, or enemies of the faith.

- [ ] **Public Performance:** Some demand perfection and happiness at all times. Religious activities, such as attending church, come with extreme demands, excessive expectations, and rigidity.
- [ ] **Authority:** Strict adherence to the abuser's rules and regulations are commanded with absolute statements about insignificant issues such as hair color or style. Non-compliance is met with severe discipline and even excommunication.
- [ ] **Segregation:** Some groups will use secrecy or withhold information from all but a few select and "worthy" individuals. Estrangement from extended family members and friends outside of the religion is not uncommon. That includes shunning, alienation, or persecution.
- [ ] **Blind Obedience:** Some abusers replace God with themselves and expect people to worship them.
- [ ] **Abuse of Authority:** Some abusers use their position or authority to connive for their personal benefit, which is often financial. They justify the behavior by saying they deserve it.
- [ ] **Fraud:** Some abusers engage in criminal misconduct or cover up the transgressions of others in the name of their religion. This includes covering up sexual abuse, physical abuse, and financial felonies and misdemeanors.
- [ ] **Other:** _____

_____

Checklist: Verbal Abuse

- [ ] **Extremes in Volume and Tone Voice:** One way is to increase their volume by yelling, screaming, and raging. The second is complete silence, ignoring, and refusing to respond.
- [ ] **Intimidating Words:** The abuser swears and uses threatening language when you refuse to do what they want.
- [ ] **Intense Manner of Speech:** This is argumentative, competitive, sarcastic, and demanding. The abuser frequently interrupts or

talks over the victim, withholds key information, bullies, and interrogates.

☐ **Personal Attacks:** Common examples include criticizing, name-calling, mocking responses, defaming character, berating feelings, and judging opinions.

☐ **No Apology:** The abuser refuses to take responsibility, becomes hostile, invalidates or dismisses your feelings, lies, and conveniently forgets promises or commitments.

☐ **Blame Game:** To the abuser, anything that goes wrong is *your* fault. The abuser accuses you of being too sensitive, is overly critical of your reactions, one-ups your feelings, and opposes your opinions.

☐ **Browbeating:** Typical sayings include: "If only you would. . . , then I wouldn't have to be this way," "You don't know how to take a joke," "The problem with you is. . . "

☐ **Other:** _____
_____

The nineteenth-century nursery rhyme "Sticks and stones may break my bones, but words will never hurt me" is not true for most people. Some people have the natural ability to emotionally disconnect when being insulted, while many of us do not. Words have meaning, and they can be hurtful.

How can the victim combat the abuse? By avoiding retaliation, whether verbal or physical. The abuser will only accuse the victim of "starting it" and will play the victim card, causing the true victim to retreat even further as the abuser gains even more control.

As a result of the verbal abuse, the victim feels they can't ever win, but that is not true. There is a better way. Even small victories are helpful and can increase self-confidence. Use these explanations to regain self-awareness.

The following list provides an opportunity to explore, evaluate, and discuss any of these thirty-five potentially destructive statements.

1. You *never* do what I ask. (Or, You are *always* out of control.) *This is an absolute statement that is designed to intimidate.*
2. If only you would . . . , then I wouldn't have to get angry. (Or, "You make me feel so angry.") *This is blame-shifting.*
3. Just do it my way, and everything will be fine. *This is intimidation.*
4. I only hurt you because you hurt me first. *This is blame-shifting and not taking responsibility.*
5. I do this (abuse) because I love you. *This is twisting the truth.*
6. This is our little secret; no one needs to know. (Or, This (abuse) is a family matter; no one needs to know about it.) *This is alienation and isolation.*
7. You can't leave until I say so. *This is restraint and intimidation.*
8. If you don't . . . , I'm going to kill you. *This is endangerment and threatening.*
9. You deserve to be hit. *This is aggression and shaming.*
10. This (abuse) is for your own good. (Or, I know what is best for you, and you don't.) *This is demeaning, manipulation, and twisting the truth.*
11. Your family or friends can't be trusted—you can only trust me. *This is isolation.*
12. You misheard me—I would never say that you are crazy. (Or, You have a bad memory; I know what really happened.) *This is gaslighting.*
13. I'll talk to you when you have done what I asked you to do. *This is passive-aggressive.*
14. I'm stronger/more powerful/smarter than you. *This is intimidation and manipulation.*
15. I will hurt myself if you leave me. *This is threatening and endangerment.*
16. It's your fault that we are in this mess, not mine. *This is projection.*
17. If you don't have sex with me, then I'll have to have it with someone else. (Or, I have to have sex, and it's your duty to give it to me.) *This is coercion and threatening infidelity.*

18. You don't deserve the things I give you. *This is browbeating and demeaning.*
19. Just do this one (sexually degrading) thing one time, and then I'll be satisfied. *These are selfish appeals.*
20. A good wife or husband would do this for me. *This is guilt-tripping and shaming.*
21. I don't owe you an apology. *This is refusing to accept responsibility and not apologizing.*
22. I'm the one who feels (angry); you can't feel that way. *This is playing the victim card.*
23. You are such a . . . (degrading name). *This is name-calling.*
24. You should be ashamed of yourself; I'm not like that at all. *This is shaming.*
25. If you don't . . . , I'll leave (divorce) you. *This is extortion.*
26. You can't go back to school (work); you are not smart enough. *This is financial abuse.*
27. No one will ever love you as I do. *This is alienation.*
28. You can't manage money, so I have to keep you out of the accounts. *This is forbidden access.*
29. I'm in control of you, even at work. *This is dominating, isolating, and controlling.*
30. The only way I can get your attention is to hit you (or throw things at you, get angry). *This is aggression.*
31. I lied to protect you. *This is confusion and twisting the truth.*
32. You have to do what I say; God said so. *This is spiritual abuse.*
33. It's not my fault that you are hypersensitive. *This is inciting insecurity and blame-shifting.*
34. No one could forgive you for what you have done. *This is shaming and isolating.*
35. You don't hear me when I talk in a normal voice. *This is using the tone of voice to intimidate.*

Each of these statements can be easily misconstrued as truth, especially if you struggle with low self-esteem or are accustomed to abuse. That's why I've laid these out in black and white—so you can increase your awareness and be prepared when the next round of insults are hurled your way.

Reminder: These checklists are starting points to bring about discussion. There are many more ways a person can be abused, so do not feel alone if you do not find the exact type of abuse listed here.

Other types can feel personal, yet they occur at a much larger level. For example, while racial abuse may be personal, it's part of a bigger problem. There's also government abuse of people's rights, which we didn't address. While we're not trying to include all examples, that doesn't mean these abuses are any less real.

Now, let's turn the page and begin the process of healing from abuse.

PART THREE

Abuse Exiled

How to Heal from Abuse

Chapter Six

Rewriting Your Story

CHANGING TRANSFORMATION

As a therapist, I believe that all people, regardless of their age, diagnosis, history, and trauma, are capable of true change. Of course, I'd be out of a job if I didn't believe that. My belief is based on evidence, after personally witnessing thousands of people turning their lives and relationships around as the results of making therapeutic changes. True transformation doesn't happen in a moment, but awareness can. Real, long-lasting change occurs through a process that begins with awareness and moves to reflection, followed by a dedication to change with determination and consistency. That can take years or even a lifetime to be fully realized.

Still, some people do not change. Whether it is a conscious or subconscious resistance, the refusal to change is still a choice. Perhaps the person receives a benefit from their disorder or dysfunction; or they are unwilling to see how their behavior impacts others; or they have embraced their dysfunction to the point of liking it. This is often seen in extreme personality disorders. Remember, at the foundation of a personality disorder is an inaccurate perception of reality, so real change is extremely difficult. Yet, it can be seen in milder roles such as dependency, codependency, passive-aggressive, or victimization. Change is possible, but it is very difficult and most likely a lifelong journey.

> **CODEPENDENCY**—EXCESSIVE emotional or psychological reliance on a partner, typically one who requires support on account of an illness, personality disorder, or addiction. A codependent boosts their ego from "helping" others at the expense of self.

> **PASSIVE-AGGRESSIVE**—DENOTING a type of behavior or personality characterized by indirect resistance to the demands of others and an avoidance of direct confrontation, as in procrastinating, pouting, avoiding problems, blaming others, hiding anger, making excuses, or misplacing important materials.

Then there are some people who fake change. This is a manipulative action done to gain some benefit, whether it be a lifestyle or a person, or something with intrinsic value, such as money, power, or influence. False change is commonly seen with addicts. Remember, a person can be addicted to a variety of substances, such as illegal drugs, prescription drugs, alcohol, caffeine, or food, or behaviors like sex, playing video games, shopping, work, and exercise. Faking change is done to deceive (intentionally and unintentionally) others that they are now different and can be trusted again. The desire is to regain immediate trust without substantial time put in. This is why we say that real change is only noticeable six months to a year after a person makes the proclamation.

So, what does real change look like? Change is not a straight line upward; rather, it is a crooked line with minor detours and setbacks. A person who has changed is upfront about their shortcomings, willing to be held accountable for their behavior, and looking for ways to improve themselves. They don't blame others for their faults but take full responsibility for their actions and behavior. They are willing to be patient with loved ones who might have a hard time trusting them again. And they are consistently pursuing a better version of themselves.

It is impossible to talk about abuse without talking about change. In order to impact the next generation, the current generations need to take a long look at themselves. What kind of abuse did you experience? How was this abuse passed down from one generation to another? In what ways did you advance the abuse, through either silence or becoming abusive?

It is only after we decide to change that healing can take place. Healing, like change, is a process that starts with a decision. Change is not a one-time event but rather a continuation of that decision. As we grow and mature, it becomes easier to see even the subtlest abuse and how it can transform an individual—regardless of your age. The effects of abuse linger and shape us into who we become. However, the processes of identifying abuse and following the suggestions in this book can truly lead to positive change.

Once we've decided to change, we need to take action. Here's one thing you can do right now that will help break the ties of abuse in your life.

REWRITING YOUR STORY

Realizing that I cannot personally meet everyone who may pick up this book, I want to give you a powerful exercise that will help you manage the *facts, feelings, and fears* around each case of abuse you'd like to address. Anyone can do this exercise. All you need are a pen and paper to keep a journal. You also can refer to the earlier sections outlining abuses and behaviors from your family tree (Chapter 5).

If you give this a legitimate shot, you will honestly begin to see change in your thoughts, emotions, and, eventually, actions. Even better, there's nothing like having a licensed therapist in your corner.

Day 1: Identify the Abuse

We've spent the whole book helping you identify the variety of abuses you may have experienced. But I'm sure there's at least one example that has recurring trauma-like effects in your life. For this exercise, select an example that would rate a 5 in terms of difficulty on a scale of 1 to 10. Why? Let's learn the process and practice on a slightly less volatile issue and attack the more difficult ones later.

Remember, it's just you, your pen, and journal. Rewriting your story begins now. For the next four consecutive days (within reason), we're going to begin to transform. Here's how:

Write It Out

Take at least fifteen minutes to an hour now (or today) to *write out your story of abuse*—not your entire life story. You may set a timer to help you focus during this exercise. Before shrugging this off or cringing like it's some school assignment, this is the WORK that is involved in breaking the ties. I didn't say it was going to be easy, but it will be helpful.

Nobody is grading you on your writing, and for the artists, you can begin to draw out your story. The only caveat for artists is that you must use the same medium every day, in this case a pencil or pen sketch. Do not switch to painting on Day 2 or to sculpture on Day 3. The purpose is to revisit the incident(s) and give your brain a chance to sort the *facts, feelings, and fears*. So, artists will be tasked with re-drawing the same incident, or related ones, each day, using the same medium.

If it's helpful, imagine writing a letter, but let your stream of consciousness flow through the pen, keyboard, or pencil. Say whatever you want, how you want. Don't worry about grammar, punctuation, commas, or complete sentences—unless you want to. It literally can be just a collection of bullet points. Just write it the way that it comes to your brain. That's the most important part. Don't reread it. Don't edit it. Just let it flow. Don't worry about chronology. Don't worry about organization. Don't even worry about whether it makes sense.

Within this framework, you might start with including the details about the timeline, *facts* about the generational, conditional, or circumstantial influences, and who was involved. Or you might vent out your frustrations by using your words any way you like.

For example, let's take a look at a case of physical abuse by a parent. You have seen or experienced being beaten, bullied, or otherwise harmed directly, which was the overt abuse that left temporary bruises but permanent emotional scars. In this process, you realized that the covert abuse was the parent's alcoholism, which runs through the family, fracturing many of the branches in the family tree.

Another example may be a case of verbal abuse. Perhaps you've discovered that your self-esteem has been affected negatively because of all the belittling you received at home, from a co-worker, or from a coach. Take one example that you recall, and use that for your first day.

Day 2: Write It Out (Again)

Open your journal to a new page, and DO NOT read what you wrote or sketched yesterday. I want your memory pathways to start fresh, and dig a little deeper, this time identifying the *feelings* surrounding the abuse, exploring additional details that are often overlooked because of suppressing the memories. Write the story out, even if parts seem repetitive. That forces our memory to pull open the file folder in our head and look at it from another perspective. This time, you may find your memory veering to how you felt the day before, during, and after the abuse, including facts that remind you of those feelings.

Day 3: Write It Out (Again)

No, it's not the movie *Groundhog Day* all over again, but I want you to turn the page again, and not re-read what you wrote previously. Your brain already knows what you've written over the last two days. Today, think through your story, and rewrite it, allowing your conscious and subconscious mind to pull up material that matters. For example, on the first day, you focused on the **facts** and timeline. The second day, you focused on your **feelings**. Today, write your story from the perspective of your **fears**, and how they influenced the situation and your life. Again, these are guidelines, not rules. The exercise is repeated for therapeutic reasons, and you may recall something you that haven't considered in the prior two days.

Day 4: Review and Rewrite IT Out (Last Time)

KINDNESS—NOUN, the quality of being friendly, generous, and considerate. Intentional kindness is different from naive kindness. Naive kindness makes you a target for further abuse. Intentional kindness is a combination of wisdom, awareness, intuition, empathy, and discernment. The Good Samaritan is an excellent example.

Today, or this week if you need a day or two of rest from the exercise, I'd like you to flip back to Day 1 and read all the way through the past few days' writings. Notice the differences. Notice the "whole" picture. What did you walk away with at the time? For example, did you decide to never drink, never hit a woman, or never raise your voice? Now, write out the story, one last time, but this time, focus on what you've learned.

By now, just by rewriting your story, you may have found some closure, or new perspective, in the process of breaking the ties to this abuse. If not, that's okay, too. We're not necessarily looking for that. But what we are looking for is an authentic, transparent view of the incident, a new depiction from several angles. That's why we need to write this out one last time. Start from the beginning, and this time, start with the end in mind. From this exercise, and perhaps with a new perspective, how would you tell the story now?

Remember how I changed my story? See below, and try to bridge the past with your new perspective. Example:

FACTS (OLD STORY)	NEW STORY
I was a victim of abuse.	Abuse is in my past, but it does not define me.
I was hurt by abuse I didn't even realize.	I've learned that I can stop the abuse in my life.
I hurt others.	My past helps me help others.
I made bad decisions.	I learned to adapt and work hard with balance.

FACTS (OLD STORY)	NEW STORY

BE A TIE-BREAKER

While giving our story a new perspective, it's likely we still need to break the mental, emotional, and even physical ties we have to the abuse and abuser.

Different therapeutic techniques like cognitive behavioral therapy, dialectical behavioral therapy, and emotion-focus therapy may be helpful. There's always a way, but there's really no exclusive way. It's highly personal to you. Regardless of how we proceed, I know that one thing is necessary to fully heal from past abuse:

We must learn to *break the ties* that abuse has on us!

For instance, we have "mental ties" from the past. From the earlier example using the alcoholic parent who was physically abusive, did you walk away saying that you would never drink, as a result of having experienced that? What promises did you make to yourself, that you might be holding on to, at a conscious and subconscious level, that might actually be causing you more harm now? Some people say things like, "I will never put myself in that situation again." Then when they kind of fall into a similar situation, all of a sudden, they react in a very angry, rageful, almost violent manner. It's so uncharacteristic of them. It's often coming from the fact that they've made some kind of promise to themselves, while their subconscious mind holds on to it at a deep level, and it's actually keeping them from healing and moving forward in a healthy way.

Once you've realized these ties—all of these things that you've been holding on to—then you have to break them to achieve a sense of freedom. From your story, we can identify the ties to abuse, as well as promises made from the abuse, and rewrite them with a new perspective. For example, maybe you don't have to give up drinking altogether. But getting drunk is not an option either. So, the new promise gives you freedom that you may not have felt before.

There's an old saying in Proverbs that says, "Be careful of the promises that you make." I used to think this referred to promises that you make to other people, or even to God. But every day that passes, the more I realize that the promises we make to ourselves are the most critical. While our entire being tries to go forward with these limitations, the whole world is fighting back, and we can get stuck. That's why we have those outbursts of frustration and anger that are just seemingly impulsive and uncharacteristic. But really, there is something behind that.

RELEASING EMOTIONAL TIES

Often we carry the burden of emotional ties that weigh us down mentally and emotionally to the point that our body starts to reflect the pain. You may literally have a "pain in the neck" because of an emotional tie or promise you've made based on a previous abuse.

Breaking emotional ties is different from breaking mental ties. In rewriting your story, on Day 2 you were guided to think about the feelings related to the abuse. Were you able to identify a feeling or emotion that you've been hanging on to? Sometimes, we may know what the problem is, but we have a somatic—or bodily—response to an emotional trigger that causes physical pain.

Now, here's the psychology behind what I just walked you through. There's a great book called *The Body Keeps the Score,* by Bessel Van der Kolk, M.D. The concept behind it is that when you go through a trauma, your body reacts in certain ways. It actually physically holds on to the trauma that you've experienced. It's much like the instant response we give before touching a hot stove. Our body remembers the last time it felt like it burned, so we instantly, automatically pull back in a twitch.

Right now, you may notice a pain flare-up, perhaps in your shoulder. I want you to acknowledge the pain or tension related to this emotional event.

Take your hand, and reach for the pain, skin on skin. Take a couple of deep breaths. Close your eyes, and imagine the event, and tell yourself, "I am safe," while deeply breathing. Now speak to the pain you're holding, thanking your body for holding on to that memory. But tell it that it doesn't need to store the memory in that physical space anymore—that it is able to release it and to let it go. You don't have to physically hold on to this trauma any longer. Then you take another deep breath, and you release it. You will actually feel a physical relief in your body.

Continue breathing, and think about the person who abused you, and speak to that pain saying you are thankful for reminding you, but you are ready to release that pain.

If this exercise is difficult, you might not be comfortable feeling difficult emotions. Feelings are neither good nor bad, right nor wrong. It is the actions we take in combination with those emotions that can make the difference. Remember, it is okay to feel difficult emotions.

ESTABLISH HEALTHY BOUNDARIES

The last part of the process, following the efforts to break the ties from the past, is to set healthy boundaries going forward.

Once we've broken the ties, and we can see things more clearly, we've remembered the event, and we've allowed it to be removed from our bodies and from our minds. The next thing is actually setting normal, healthy boundaries going forward with this person, if they are still in your life. For example, with the abusive, alcoholic parent, you might decide to avoid talking with them when they are drinking.

If you find it difficult to think of a healthy boundary in your situation, try asking yourself the question differently: "What advice would you give a friend of yours, who told you the same story?" "What would you say to a friend of yours, who said, 'I went through this abuse as a child'?"

Many times it's easier to help judge someone else's situation than our own. Then, think about how that advice would apply to your situation. Your own advice could be useful, or it could at least begin the thought process of what the boundary may look like in your own life.

But safety and security are always job number one. So, if you fear the worst, and the abuser is unrepentant after being confronted before, then you will need to establish very firm boundaries, perhaps with the help of the courts. If anyone (therapist, friend, parent) is telling you that your abuser is dangerous, please listen. A client of mine was mildly assaulted by her husband, and I warned her not to go back to him. She did. The next abuse was worse, resulting in her hospitalization.

Remember the cycle of abuse? When you return to your abuser after an event, they become emboldened and will escalate the behavior. Don't trust the abuser's self-assessment of change, talk to their therapist and see if the change is real or not. This is another example of a healthy boundary.

Healthy boundaries become like skin on your body. They hold everything together, while giving your muscles, skeletal system, and bloodstream a chance to operate properly. Without skin, or boundaries, you would fall apart and be more susceptible to viruses, like abuse. Healthy boundaries hold everything in a place while protecting you from harm and danger.

BOUNDARY SPECTRUM

Banishing	Not recommended, unless there are serious threats to well-being.
Limiting contact	Allowing supervised contact under strict conditions (time periods).
Controlled contact	Allowing supervised contact more frequently.
Unsupervised contact	Allowing short time periods of contact without supervision.
Extended contact	Allowing more time for unsupervised contact.
All-access	Under guidelines, all parties agree to mutual, respectable contact.

From there, the time, frequency, and levels of supervision may increase or decrease as necessary. This spectrum example is a guideline. But healthy boundaries may be as simple and direct as "I won't speak with you until you are ninety days clean and sober." I've included several more examples in the next chapter, "How to Confront Abuse."

THE SAMARITAN'S EXAMPLE

One famous Bible story told by Jesus is about the Good Samaritan, but most people relate to the beaten man instead of to what we can learn from how the Samaritan intervened to help the trauma of abuse. While the Bible does teach people to love their neighbor, in this story it also teaches *how*.

As you may recall, the story begins with a man who is beaten, robbed, and left for dead. Laying on the side of the road, two different people pass by without doing anything for the abused man. Then, a Samaritan walks by. Despite cultural rules, he leans into the healing process with healthy boundaries.

Consider this:

1. First, the Samaritan brings the abused to an inn. Notice that he doesn't bring him to his place of work, and he doesn't bring him to his house. He brings the man to a third location, for which he doesn't have any kind of vested interest, and for safekeeping.

2. Next, the Samaritan doesn't give the money to the abused. He gives it to the innkeeper. The innkeeper becomes in charge of how much care that person needs. The Samaritan tells the innkeeper to be the one to judge, whether or not more care is required or more money needs to be spent. The Samaritan doesn't give these rights to the abused man, because the abused man might not be in his right mind.

What's clever about this story is that Jesus teaches to show love to strangers, but also within healthy boundaries. The Samaritan protects his home by taking the injured man to an inn. He serves the injured man by giving money to the innkeeper, and delegating a third party to determine his needs. Of the many lessons here, one is that it's not our job to heal someone, but we can lead them wisely. *Everyone is responsible for their own healing.*

This process for healing from the abuse can be repeated with other abuses in your life, but don't rush it. Take the time you need in each case, and don't force yourself to try to do too much at once. Remember, healing takes time, and your mind and body need to process the changes, break the ties, and see where healthy boundaries can be established.

Chapter Seven

How to Confront Abuse

Confronting an abusive person is never easy, especially when it's a spouse, parent, employer, or child, and the relationship is not easily banished. Sometimes the abuse is so intense that the relationship must be dissolved for the safety of the victim. Other times, the abuse may be mild but nonetheless is hurtful and harmful in several ways.

Remember, the abuser might not be aware of their abusive behavior, so it is important that they, too, be given a chance to change. Here are some suggestions for handling abusive people:

1. **See It.** There are many ways a person can be abused, as discussed in Chapter 5. Begin to see the different examples for what they are: abuse. This can be done long after the abuse has occurred, or even while it is occurring.

2. **Speak It.** This step requires quite a bit of courage and strength, but it is easier after you have walked through the previous chapter's steps of healing. In the moment of an abusive encounter, say to yourself what kind of abuse is happening. Repeat this exercise over and over to gain the necessary

bravery before confronting your abuser. When ready, speak to your abuser in a calm voice, not a harsh tone. (There is no benefit to be gained by being just as abusive as an abuser.) The intent is to bring awareness to the abuser that they are being abusive and to allow them to back off or save face. Here are a few examples of how to address the abuser:

A. "You are physically restraining me by blocking the door."

B. "That stare is not going to intimidate me."

C. "It is not okay for you to call me that name."

D. "I am not embarrassed by that story."

3. **Stress It.** If the previous step does not work, try this: As your abuser shatters your newly expressed boundaries, begin by saying, "I'm not going to take this anymore." Now is the time to add more weight to the previous statements by letting your abuser know there will be consequences for violating your personal boundaries. Here are a couple of examples:

A. **Physical Boundary:** "No one is going to touch me in a threatening manner.

   (1) Consequence: "This relationship is over if you physically try to harm me."

B. **Mental Boundary:** "I'm not going to tolerate an implication that I'm crazy."

   (1) Consequence: "I'm not listening to this accusation, and I'm walking away."

C. **Oral Boundary:** "I'm not going to shout just because someone else is."

   (1) Consequence: "Either you speak to me in a normal tone, or we will not speak at all."

D. **Emotional Boundary:** "I won't be guilt-tripped into doing something."

   (1) Consequence: "You cannot make me feel guilty, and I will not do something out of fear."

4. **Stand By It.** Once a consequence has been stated, it must be carried out if the abuse continues. Otherwise, your abuser will just intensify the abuse next time. It is important to have a friend or family member hold you accountable for your boundary-setting and enforcement. That gives you the much-needed support when you are the victim again and being attacked by your abuser.

The only way abuse stops is if you stand up to it. While that is difficult, it is not impossible. The result is the possibility of living free from abusive behavior, and that will benefit your mental, emotional, and physical well-being.

When you stand up to your abuser, it will feel awkward and uncomfortable at first, because you are breaking mental ties in your brain that previously accepted this abuse as normal. Instead, you are establishing new healthy boundaries. New healthy pathways in the brain require consistency and patience to develop properly. Be kind to yourself during this period, and surround yourself with supportive family and friends.

Next, let's look at how to be kind to others who have suffered abuse.

HOW TO TALK TO A VICTIM OF RAPE

The numerous sexual assault cases that stemmed from the #MeToo movement have reignited old stereotypes about rape and abuse. Some new acquaintances of mine, who were unaware of my vocation, commented on their dissatisfaction with the outing of several public figures. Rather than argue my position, I chose to listen to a barrage of ignorance and blame-casting. After all, my primary job is to listen and begin from a place of understanding. However, even I found that diffi-cult to achieve with comments that reeked of judgment and prejudice.

Their comments, like "Why did they wait so long?" or "So what if he is a public figure—they should have told someone," and "They are just out for the money," were filled with shame and blame for the victims. This judgmental attitude is exactly what keeps many victims from coming forward. A better understanding of the process, more safety for the victims, patience, and consistent prosecution of the abusers are needed.

The following describes the process that many victims experience from incidents of rape to the unfortunate decision to be silent. I've offered some suggestions for each step so you or someone you know can be more supportive and less judgmental.

The Shock. An experienced rapist has the pattern down. They begin by targeting a naïve and unsuspecting victim, grooming them unknowingly for a future attack. The rapist has planned out everything well in advance and tests the victim's vulnerability in advance. Like leading cattle to the slaughter, the abuser takes their time by minimizing any fear and attacking when least expected. Most victims say the whole experience happens so quickly, they hardly have time to catch up mentally, as their thoughts race, and fear consumes them.

> *Empathy. The rapist has the upper hand in that they know what they want and have the determination to move forward. The victim is unaware of the surprise attack until afterward. Most victims have a trusting nature and are not anticipating the potential harm. Empathy should be expressed for the victim any time they communicate their story. Each time they share, it is a reminder of their naiveté and pain.*

The Exit. Those victims who were lucky enough to escape their abusers are often so disoriented from the experience that they have a hard time even knowing what the next step is. Feeling disgusted, violated, and frightened, they often do the first simple thing that comes to mind: Wash to feel clean. It is natural to feel dirty as a result of this crime. Unfortunately, washing can erase evidence and can make proving things more difficult later. But the executive-function part of the brain is not operational during periods of heightened stress, so logic escapes as desperation settles in.

Awareness. The mind-body connection is real. When the body is under attack, the mind goes into survival mode with an automatic reaction of fight, flight, freeze, or faint. Frequently, victims report seeing limited possibilities of how to survive and not being able to fully process what is happening. This is why they have a difficult time assessing the situation and making wise choices.

The Abuse Pattern. All too often, the initial abuse experience is only the beginning. Afterward, there are countless narratives of the event to people who are rarely helpful and frequently judgmental. Monday-night quarterbacking picks apart every tiny decision and usually results in blaming the victim. Then others, both knowingly and unknowingly, make insensitive and ignorant remarks, which will re-traumatize the victim yet again. That causes them to shut down completely.

Kindness. "I would have done it differently" is not helpful, and it is cruel. The fact that a person is alive after an assault is a victory. Opening compassionate arms, allowing the victim to feel safe after a trauma, is the kindest of acts. That does more for the healing process than any other therapeutic technique.

The Outcome. The previous point is precisely why many victims choose silence over the additional condescending glances and unfair sentences. Of course, that means the abuser is free to do the same act to others, since they didn't receive any consequences for their actions. That reality adds to the guilt and burden, not of the rapist, but of the victim. It is not until one person breaks the silence that others follow along with relief and horror that they were not the only ones.

Closure. There is no forgetting. That is why victims can recount the event with such great detail many years later, for it is etched in the foundation of their being. Some are able to forgive their attackers, others are not. There should be no judgment for those who are unable to forgive. But a scar is left, remaining for life.

My hope is to silence judgmental opinions while voicing hope and compassion for victims. After all, judgment should be reserved for the abusive behavior, not for the victim's response.

Now, let's look at some practical strategies for confronting your abuser, using verbal abuse for the context.

STRATEGIES FOR COMBATING VERBAL ABUSE

Words have meaning, and they can hurt you.

This is precisely what the abuser is depending on: To hurt you with their hurt. Once harmed, you are easier to control and manipulate. With one well-placed phrase, the abuser disarms you and gains dominance without ever touching you. This very effective abuse method is commonly seen in work, family and/or community relationships.

How can the victim combat verbal abuse? Not by retaliating with verbal insults, that's for sure. The reason is because often the abuser will point the finger back at *you*, acting as if *they* are being victimized. That causes you to retreat even further, and the abuser gains even more control.

There is a better way. For each of the verbal attacks listed below, try one of these strategies instead:

- *Abusers use the volume and tone of their voice, either by yelling or ignoring, to establish dominance.* Resist the urge to scream or give the silent treatment. Instead, go to the middle ground, and stay there. If your abuser yells, respond in a pleasant voice slightly quieter than normal. If they ignore that, speak to them anyway. Pretend they are responding, and continue the conversation in a calm manner.

- *Abusers use swearing and threatening language to instill fear, intimidate, manipulate, oppress, and constrain.* When attacked in this manner, strong positive self-talk is essential. Say to yourself, *I am not afraid* or *They can't make me do anything*, over and over. This is not something to be said out loud, rather it's repeated inside your head. Two things are accomplished: First, you'll feel better, and second, you won't be tempted to respond to the threat from a position of weakness or survival mode.

- *The abuser's manner of speech is argumentative, competitive, sarcastic, and demanding.* When they go into this mode, stop speaking until they are done. Take a deep breath, and think to yourself, *There they go again*, which helps to neutralize the behavior in your mind. Then decide how much the conversation topic means to you. The degree to which it matters to you will determine your level of response. If it doesn't really matter in the grand scheme of things, there's no reason to antagonize them further. If it does matter to you, then my default response advice is: *Do not* address what they are saying and follow the conversation down a rabbit hole to a no-win situation. Instead, react with a "politician moment," answering the question you wished they had asked. If they don't hear you or acknowledge your questions, or if their speech gets more intense, you can say, "I can see this is getting serious. I want to take a break and continue this later when we're both calmer." You don't want to get into a verbal altercation, and you don't want them to feel "exposed." Be self-protective, that's job number one. Most importantly, don't tell the abuser how much it hurts you, because that might be what they want.

- *Abusers use personal attacks such as name-calling, mocking responses, defaming character, berating feelings, and judging opinions.* This condemning tactic leaves you feeling inferior and defeated. Again, counteract this with positive self-talk and the truth. It might sound overly simplistic, but it is highly effective. Do a reality check by running each personal attack through a best-friend test: Would a best friend agree with the insult? No. Therefore, there is no validity to the verbal assault.

- *Abusers, become hostile, invalidate or dismiss feelings, lie, refuse to take responsibility, and conveniently forget promises or commitments.* Everyone is responsible for their own actions and responses. Victims tend to take on more than their own fair share of the abuse by making excuses, thus letting the abuser off the hook. When the abuser is faced with a real-life consequence for their verbal assaults, don't bail them out.

- *Typical abusive sayings include:* "I'm critical for your own good," "I was only joking when I said that...," "If only you would..., then I wouldn't have to be this way," "You don't know how to take a joke," "The problem with you is...," and "That (verbal abuse) didn't really happen." These phrases are signals that a verbal-abuse rant is about to begin. Use them as warning signs, and get out of the conversation as quickly as possible. This is a great time to become distracted by something or someone outside of the conversation.

As a result of the verbal abuse, sometimes you feel that you can't ever win, but that is not true. Even small victories are helpful and can increase self-confidence. Use these strategies to regain self-esteem. Then make a decision about when and how to get away from your abuser.

HOW TO HANDLE ABUSE: BEFORE/DURING/AFTER

In the examples below, neither one wants to be in an abusive relationship, and each is in the process of actively looking for ways out of their situation.

Mark's wife began by verbally abusing him early on in the marriage. As the years progressed, so did her abusive behavior. It escalated into her throwing things and destroying his phone. He wants to get a divorce, but he also wants to wait until after his daughter graduates from high school, which is about one year away. But his wife's behavior only gets worse as time goes on. He doesn't know why or what causes it, but he feels he has to endure it, buying time for his daughter to graduate.

❅ ❅ ❅ ❅ ❅

Natalie's boss is overbearing, demanding, sexually harassing, and downright rude. Even though she has reported some of his abusive behavior to Human Resources, he still manages to escape any consequences. Because she is a single parent, she needs the income and cannot quit her job until she has another one lined up. She is in a horrible situation, with no other source of income, and the object of constant sexual harassment. The boss justifies his behavior by saying, "You're being overly dramatic." She feels like she doesn't have a choice. She has to stay until she finds another job, and she doesn't want to leave on bad terms. She asked me, "How do I handle my everyday life, without losing my mind or losing my job?"

Not everyone is able to leave their abuser immediately, as is the case for Mark and Natalie. So, how can they, or you, survive until escape is possible? Try these methods:

Before the abuse starts:

- *Learn about kinds of abuse:* There are several types of abuse, as we outlined earlier, so become familiar with them so you can recognize them. For example, Mark experienced physical (aggression, hitting, throwing objects), emotional (guilt tripping, anger rages, confusion), and verbal (name-calling, belittling, sarcasm) abuse, while Natalie experienced financial (threats of losing her job, reducing her pay), mental (gaslighting, twisting the truth, silent treatment), and sexual (grooming, coercion, inciting fear) abuse.
- *Know the person:* Mark and Natalie began to study their abusers from the outside, looking in on their situations. That perspective allowed them to see their abusers as tormented souls who needed help from someone other than them.
- *Anticipate type of abuse:* The combination of knowing the types of abuse and studying an abuser, allows you to be able to anticipate the type of abuse more accurately. Most abusers use the same tactics over and over, so it is not too difficult to spot.

Anticipating a potentially abusive situation allows you to look at the abuse strategically, instead of emotionally.

- *Set reasonable expectations:* Instead of believing that the abuse would stop, Mark and Natalie began to realize that their abusers would likely look for other targets if they were not there. Unless a person goes through a significant transformation, abusive behavior is not likely to change.

During the abuse:

- *Put on a protective bubble:* Think of the bubble as an invisible force field that no one can penetrate. A person inside the bubble can see outside it, just as a person outside the bubble can see inside. However, there is a protective layer that keeps the abuser's emotions from penetrating the bubble, and that's how it protects the person inside from absorbing the abuse.
- *Slow speech down, and talk in a quiet voice:* One of the most natural methods to make an abusive person calm down quickly is to slow down the rate of speaking and talk in a hushed voice. This method almost forces the abuser to match the new speed instead of escalating.
- *Pause for extra breaths:* The slower speech allows for deep breathing. This oxygenates the whole body while giving the brain extra time to process. At first, this is difficult, but with practice, it becomes easier.
- *Lower heart rate:* After slowing the speech and adding more breaths, it is more natural to become aware of an elevated heart rate. Be intentional about slowing it down. This lessens the intensity from increased anxiety as a result of the abuse.
- *Say, "I'm safe":* The normal response to an abusive moment is to go into survival mode. But that leads to a "fight, flight, freeze, or faint" response. Once it is activated, the brain shuts down, and the response is automated, leaving no room for executive functioning. Instead, say the words, "I am safe," which will prevent the survival mode from activating.

- *Countdown "5, 4, 3, 2, 1, I'm present":* Mark and Natalie discovered that the defense mechanism of dissociation happened during abusive moments. While this can be useful in some instances, not being present meant they were shutting down and often wished they said something but couldn't seem to think of it. Counting down by saying, "5, 4, 3, 2, 1, I'm present" kept them in the present and disconnected from their typical defense mechanisms.

After the abusive behavior:

- *Don't over-assess the incident:* There is nothing good that comes after reviewing an abusive moment excessively. That can lead to absorbing harmful information, and/or believing the lies of the abuser. There will be a time when you can do the "Write It Out" exercise explained earlier, replaying the incident through the lens of facts, feelings, and fears. But the point is to avoid dwelling on the abuse. Instead, learn from the incident, and discover ways to improve your own performance.

- *Look for ways to improve yourself:* The stronger a person is, the harder it is to abuse them. Mark and Natalie worked hard at improving their self-images, gaining confidence from environments outside of the abuse, and engaging with people who loved them.

- *Express stored emotion:* During the abusive moment, it is not wise to express any emotion. Rather, shelve it for another time, but do readdress it when in a safe location. Alone, Mark and Natalie would pretend that they were screaming at the person doing the abuse. That allowed them a chance to release their pent-up emotions.

- *Release the event:* Regardless of a person's ability to forgive an abusive event, it cannot be, and should not be, forgotten. While the event doesn't have to live in the present moment, the lessons learned from the abuse do last a lifetime. Make them valuable.

Eventually, Mark and Natalie were able to get out of their abusive situations. The skills they learned during the abuse became valuable life-altering lessons. Still, forgiveness continues to be required in order to break the emotional ties. The line "Forgive and forget," is partially true. We must forgive, but we do not need to forget the abuse, because remembering actually leads to preventing abuse in future.

HOW FORGIVENESS WORKS MAGIC

First, trying to force someone to forgive before they're ready is a terrible idea. Forgiveness is a process that takes time, hopefully transforming into a lifestyle. Here's what I mean.

While forgiveness is often prescribed as a remedy for healing from trauma, it's not easy to accomplish. Still, reaching this point can bring closure and help you move from victim to victor. Forgiveness allows you to regain control and feel empowered which undermines your abuser's influence.

Unfortunately, forgiveness is sometimes reduced to another task on the healing to-do list, instead of a true change of heart. This minimizes the full impact and reduces it to a behavioral, instead of an attitudinal, experience. Martin Luther King Jr. said it well:

"Forgiveness is not an occasional act, it is a constant attitude."

How can you forgive your abuser? And also, how do you, if you're the abuser, forgive yourself? Here are some suggestions:

1. **Understand the reason for forgiveness.** Forgiveness is not for the sake of the abuser. It is for the health of the victim. When you decide to forgive an act, you release yourself from the controlling power of the abuse. It is not something to be entered into lightly, forced upon you through manipulation, or guilt-tripped. Those ways only add to the trauma rather than healing from it. Instead, forgiveness must come from a desire to "let it go." Let go of the pain, hurt, trauma, and influence. This does not mean the abuse is forgotten, just that it has lost the power to control.

2. **Identify large areas needing forgiveness.** Accidents, traumas, abuse, disasters, addiction, and death are some of the areas where forgiveness might be needed. Each person and situation are unique, so it is unfair to project or judge what or whom should be forgiven. This is an individual choice, resting solely in your hands. Sometimes a person needs to be forgiven for an offensive act. Sometimes you need to forgive yourself. Or sometimes, there is no single person responsible, so a blanket forgiveness of a culture, religion, or sect might need to be granted.

3. **Begin a forgiveness list.** Writing down who—or what offense—needs to be, or has been, forgiven will help to bring clarity to the issues at hand. The famous Twelve Steps include one that calls for making a moral inventory of offenses, character defects. Think of it as a list divided into two main categories: those actions of others a person needs to forgive, and those actions of self in need of forgiveness. This is not a list to be distributed or shared with anyone unless in a therapeutic setting. It is only for the benefit of the person creating the list, not the benefit of others.

4. **Counteract unforgiving (obsessive) thoughts.** Are you having a hard time knowing what needs to go on the list? Look to obsessive thoughts to identify areas you revisit over and over. Anything that is replaying again and again, with no new insight or understanding, is obsessive. Other examples include envisioning anger rants, imagining horrible scenarios, having a judgmental attitude about others, pondering negative comments, and deliberating past decisions. These thoughts are indications of possible areas that still need to be forgiven.

5. **Recognize anger, frustration, anxiety, depression, or annoyance as possible indicators of emotions that arise in the absence of forgiveness.** In addition to thoughts, intense feelings can identify an area needing forgiveness. A strong emotional response to a person, event, or memory might require

more investigation as to its cause. It is normal to relive some emotion when retelling a traumatic story; however, having too much or none at all are signals that some issue needs addressing or possibly requires forgiveness.

6. **Make forgiveness a daily activity.** Adopting an attitude of forgiveness changes the way a person views life. Think of it as a positive versus a negative outlook on life. The lens through which a person views life (positive or negative) influences nearly every decision that is made. The same is true for an attitude of forgiveness. Once embraced, this determines a person's approach, opinion, temper, outlook, mindset, and reaction. It can transform a person at a deep level.

7. **Create a forgiving mantra.** "I choose forgiveness" can be a simple chant to remember when driving on a highway, listening to someone yell, or recalling a past event. Forgiving even the smallest events can bring about a sense of peace and restoration. Remember, forgiveness does not mean forgetting. Forgetting minimizes, or denies, an event rather than confronting it in a healthy way.

Having an attitude of forgiveness changes an individual's perspective on even difficult events.

However, this is not appropriate for everyone and not possible in every circumstance. Just as it is not possible to be positive in every situation, it is also not reasonable to expect a forgiving attitude for every condition.

Instead, be kind to yourself and others. After all, kindness is the antonym (or opposite) of abuse.

> **KINDNESS**—Noun, the quality of being friendly, generous, and considerate. Intentional kindness is different from naive kindness. Naive kindness makes you a target for further abuse. Intentional kindness is a combination of wisdom, awareness, intuition, empathy, and discernment. The Good Samaritan is an excellent example.

CONCLUSION

By now, I hope the word "abuse" no longer carries a scary stigma as a topic to avoid. Instead, almost like "mental illness" has become more understood, I hope abuse becomes more openly addressed so healing can occur. Additionally, I hope that by now—whether you are the abuser, the victim, both, or neither—you have identified areas that have bred disorder and dysfunction in your life and family. Most importantly, by now I hope you have found hope, help, and a path towards healing.

This may be the last chapter in the book, but it is NOT the conclusion of the journey. It's more like "passing the baton" with a pivot in a new direction. There's no end to abuse until a new baton has been passed, and the corner has been turned.

Breaking the ties and patterns in your family, and in your life, will help you pass on healthy traits with generational impact for your future grandchildren.

Regardless of the abuse, I hope by now you see that it starts with you. You are equipped and empowered to stop the abuse, repair the damage, and enjoy a healthy new relationship with those around you. Instead of pointing fingers, let's address the entire story in context, with generational, conditional, and circumstantial evidence, and learn from it instead of burying it. Let's confront it instead of withdrawing from it. And, let's do it with intentional kindness, not judgment.

There's hope for the abuser, too. You can change and transform into a better version of yourself. It's hard to forgive yourself, but it's a worthy endeavor that may keep you out of jail. Our own generational, conditional, and circumstantial factors have shaped us into who we are, but that doesn't have to be the end of our story. We can change. We can transform and live with a healthy purpose that positively impacts those around us. Life has too much good to be weighed down with bad.

Breaking the cycle of abuse requires us to take responsibility and see the facts, feelings, and fears and treat them with maturity, a clean mind, and an open heart. We will grow from this "fertilizer" that has been put in our lives, which will end up strengthening us moving forward.

First, we must be **free** from the abuse, **grow** from the experience, and **inspire** others to learn from our mistakes. It's my personal mantra: **FREE—GROW—INSPIRE.**

> *When we are **free** from the past,*
> *it is easier to **grow** in the present*
> *and then **inspire** the future.*

Freedom helps us avoid repeating the patterns of abuse, and that inspires others to walk through the process of healing. Imagine the differences in your family if they were to heal from past abuse and avoid abuse in the present, which could discontinue abuse in the future. How about at work? At school? In the neighborhood? At church? The ripple effect of healing from abuse extends for miles and years beyond what we can envision. Yet, it starts with you.

I know how hard that first step is—admitting abuse. Trust me, it gets easier as you develop your own pace for healing. The only race you are running is your own. Make it count for yourself and for your family.

WOMEN

Now, I turn to the women reading. There's a greater chance that you've been abused, and stuffed the incident(s) so deep you can't even believe it's changed you. You want to believe you've forgotten about it. Still, abuse tends to take away a piece of us. We will naturally try to fill that space, often "unintentionally," with another abusive relationship.

Domestic violence occurs more often than anyone wants to admit, and keeping the family together can become a misguided mantra.

Mothers cannot prevent their children from being affected. Growing up with abuse in the household can warp a young boy's or girl's understanding of a loving marriage. The mom often takes on so much of the protection for the kids that she often doesn't protect herself. So, while the mom tries to shield her kids from it all, the fabric of the family is being ripped apart.

Remember, you are not a product of your own production. Other influences shaped you. But you can control the power those influences have over you, moving into the future.

Today's woman has more opportunities than ever before. We can literally create a new reality for ourselves. The past is a learning ground, not a graveyard. It's meant to improve us, not weigh us down. Women have the same rights and opportunities today, yet too often abuse can hold us back.

While much abuse is overtly obvious, like physical or sexual assault, I hope we have seen how we all may have some hidden abusive traits we have never acknowledged, and how we may still have hurt others. Children are raised with their parents' belief systems, yet the parents must assess how they will raise their kids in light of their own values and priorities and today's modern world views. Some parenting practices that were normal in the past are considered abuse today—and often for good reason. Still, our children are raised under influences they cannot control, like their parents' behaviors and belief systems. What's left is a new paradigm in parenting in virtually every generation.

Women become the glue to the family. Women have the power to lead the change and transformation. Women, regardless of age, can be the driving force behind positive relationship-building, hope for a better tomorrow, and love throughout the transformation.

MEN

Unfortunately, men are usually delivering the worst part of abuse in the family. Sure, women abuse men, as we have discussed, but typically men are responsible for the good or the bad part of their family dynamics, but transforming men offers the greatest opportunity.

From an early age, boys learn cues from their fathers and friends, and from movie and sports heroes, to shape who they are and how to behave. Raising children is probably the most difficult thing to do, because men have to face their own weaknesses, and many don't have a good role model as a reference. That's not always easy for men. So, nothing changes until something happens.

If you've physically or sexually abused someone, this book can only get you so far. Additional help with healing and growing may require serious work in the therapy office. Some will never be able to forgive you. No matter how much you love or care for those you have hurt, the damage has been done and may not be repairable. That's the hole you've dug. But there's a ladder out.

Someone has to put the ladder down for you, which may be a therapist or mentor. But you have to climb out. Every rung on the ladder represents a major, personal issue you have to work through before moving up. Or you can look at the ladder and stay where you are. Rewriting Your Story will be key in processing this. Soon, you'll be able to coach yourself out of harm's way because of what you've learned, what's at stake, and how you want to live.

Many sons are raised with limited contact with their dads, if any at all. It's no wonder that many of our broken families are led by single mothers. Without mentors and father figures, our sons fight or flee to avoid dealing with truth and emotions. It's only made worse with drinking or drug use.

But men are the key to transforming our society. Men are the sleeping giants, who can be equipped to handle situations differently. Men who rise above their own problems, and lead lives that their kids will honor and respect, will transform their communities, with positive ripple effects throughout their lives.

CHILDREN

You may be the most at risk, yet with the most opportunity. Future relationships depend on how well you heal from the past, whether there was overt or covert abuse. You may have experienced abuse directly, or you may have observed abuse that has affected your point of view. You may not even realize the damage done, but you may know that something from the past is holding you back.

Honestly, adults are often less mature than children. Don't let that impact your growth. Regardless of the adults in your life, you know right from wrong. It may be hard to stand for the truth at younger ages, but it's possible. You are the future, and accepting that will help your maturity level.

Still, the pressure is not on you. The adults, including your parents, have treated you based on their own experiences. The pressure is on them. You just have to see through the drama and into a future of opportunity.

That opportunity is about your growth, also a chance to break the cycle of abuse in your family. The buck stops with you. You may be young, but you are stronger than you know.

GRANDPARENTS

We can learn from your experience, and hopefully you can, too. The more you remember the ways you were raised, and how abuse was dealt with throughout your lifetime, the better your family will be able to learn from the ups and downs. Inevitably, you've passed on traits to your children who are now parents, whether they are good or bad versions. But you can change your family's future by seeking forgiveness where it's needed, and passing the baton of forgiveness throughout the family. Forgiveness is not a switch that is flipped on, it's more of a journey of learning, growing, and being set free from past hurts. As we age, our maturity and experience often give us the ability to forgive more easily.

Grandparents who find themselves in this situation of remembering past abuse tend to be overwhelmed with guilt and grief. The guilt comes from awareness, not to beat yourself with, but to recognize what you've gone through, so you can address what you need to heal. The grief results from a feeling of a lost opportunity—recognizing what didn't happen because of what *did* happen. Regardless of age, grandparents need to work through the grief, perhaps with a counselor, and find the ability to ask for forgiveness, to be open to hear the other side of the story.

EVERY READER

As an abuser, we're not always aware of abuse, and may resist the thought that we were the problem. As the victim, your abuser might not see things the same way you do. So there has to be an allowance for how another person perceives the abuse versus how you see it. When in doubt, the victim's perception takes precedence. However, this is not a free pass to wrongfully accuse another person. That, in itself can be abusive.

Remember, not everyone will, or can, take responsibility and seek healing. Perhaps the abuser has passed away, or is not emotionally ready, or is caught in a cycle of addiction, and can't handle facing the truth. They may even refuse the conversation altogether. You have to accept that. Even if they're on their deathbed, what do you gain from confronting them at this time?

Instead, when you can't have a conversation with the person due to their circumstances, try this:

Write a letter to them, whether they are dead or alive. This letter becomes your vehicle to heal. You can write whatever you want, however you want—just unload this burden onto paper. Give it twenty-four hours before you reread it, edit it, and make sure that it is all on the paper. Next, burn it, throw it into a lake, or bury it. As it disintegrates, use this opportunity to forgive, if you are ready, and remove the emotional weight from your shoulders. This releases the pain and allows you to let it go.

During my grandmother's last days, I decided to write a letter to her so I could release all my frustration. Although she was fully cognizant, I knew she would not be able to receive it well. There was no point in making matters worse. So, I wrote the letter and later burned it to dust.

I did the same exercise with my memories with Hank. Instead of burning it, I was able to share the letter with him. Unfortunately, his response was to blame my mother for his abuse because "she deserved it." It doesn't always go well. Remember, forgiveness is for you, not your abuser. Because he was unwilling to accept any responsibility, I erected a boundary of no communication for my safety and the safety of my family.

As for my dad, instead of writing to him, I studied narcissism and learned everything I could on the subject. I don't agree with some experts that you have to eliminate every narcissist from your life. That is an impossible task given that many reach the upper echelon of their careers. But you can learn how to live, work, manage, and even love them. My podcast, *Understanding Today's Narcissist*, offers a new way of viewing narcissism, as a disability, instead of a disorder.

HOLD ON WITH FAITH

Throughout my own story of abuse, faith in God has been a "strong tower" for me to lean on when circumstances haven't made sense. The AA tradition of Twelve Steps refers to God as a Higher Power to whom we can take our burdens if we are willing to surrender them. Regardless of religion, I encourage you to explore that side of your life. Trusting in something greater than yourself helps toward understanding that life isn't just about you.

There are reasons for the abuse, and it points to helping you know your place and purpose in life, and how you fit into everything around you. For me, I know that my real Father has good plans for me and will put people into my life to accomplish a greater goal.

Nobody can force you into believing in God or Higher Power, but it's probably the single, most important decision of your life and something that can be carried with you everywhere. Forgiveness, healing from abuse, and breaking the ties can be difficult without granting mercy and grace when appropriate. This can come from God, who loved us first.

I could not wrap up this book until suggesting that if you do not have faith, find it. If you do, hold on to it. Our God, or Higher Power, loves you despite what has happened in the past. He can provide more than any therapist or brain scan.

IN CLOSING

In helping thousands of clients through abuse, I consider myself blessed. Watching people recover from significant trauma and abuse is a testimony to the resilience, determination, and hope that lie in each of us.

People who have experienced incest, sex trafficking, attempted murder, rape, or molestation at young ages, and those who have been beaten to a pulp, are examples of clients who have recovered to the point that they are living full, healthy, normal lives. You would never know they have gone through these traumas by looking at them now.

You know the heaviness of abuse that weighs on you. But after some work, the fog will clear, the weight will be lifted, and you will be better. Then you will be able to spot abuse more quickly, and not be afraid to call it out any longer. Abuse will have lost its power to subdue you. You will have safe boundaries in your life for you and your family. And finally, you will feel comfortable in your own skin. This is how you will know that you have fully healed.

For now, I encourage you to view your life with a renewed desire for healing from the pain, finding peace in the midst of chaos, recognizing the abuse, acknowledging any repercussions, and saving future generations from the trap. Get free from your past, grow in your present, and inspire the future.

Abuse is one chain that can be broken. It's a virus with an antidote and that antidote is kindness for you and others. There's hope for healing and transforming the next generation. That's why exposing abuse may be the most powerful exercise in your life.

ACKNOWLEDGMENTS

WORD OF THANKS.

The year 2020 is an unusual time to be writing a book. Unlike many who were furloughed or without employment, my private therapy practice was busier. Months of confinement led to an increase in domestic violence, anger outbursts, marriage troubles, depression, anxiety, paranoia, isolation, suicidality, and substance abuse. I heard more gut-wrenching stories of attempted murder, rape, physical abuse, threats, assaults, unwilling confinements, illnesses, drug overdoses, and deaths in a few months, than in years before. And yet, this increase both in intensity and frequency is precisely the reason for writing this book.

As a therapist, hearing these stories everyday can be overwhelming. So, during this time, I developed a new way of managing the added stress. At the end of each session, I would think about one thing I was thankful regarding my client. For instance, "I'm thankful that they are getting help," "I'm thankful that they seem to hear about boundaries," or "I'm thankful that they are healing." This simple change helped me to see each client with a renewed respect, care, and empathy.

The same level of thankfulness goes for the writing of this book. I cannot, and do not want to, do this alone. I am so grateful for everyone who has encouraged and supported me in this journey. The love you have shown me, I hope to give back by helping others who have been or will be abused.

My Family. I am blessed to have my husband, Michael, and my kids James, Jessica, Julia, and Sofiana. All of you have loved and supported me in your own way and truly am grateful for each of you. I am also blessed to have a wonderful mother who is the epitome of a modern working mom, long before it acceptable to be that way. Your dedication to your family is inspiring and words are insufficient to express my appreciation.

My Clients. Everyday you inspire me to move forward. It is an honor to see your progress and watch you transform your life and the lives around you. I am thankful that you chose me to be part of your journey.

My Friends. I have so many friends who encouraged me during this time and took an interest in what I was doing and how I was doing. Angie and Allison, both of you, went above the bar to keep me sane and I am so grateful.

My Practice. I cannot thank my office staff at Psychological Affiliates enough for the wonderful support that I receive daily. Without your help, I could not get nearly as much accomplished, let alone done well. Betsy, you are a God send. Thank you, Dr. Deborah Day, for your encouragement.

My Endorsements. To all of you who endorsed me or the book, thank you. Your backing is humbling and the time you gave to participate is so valued, I am indebted to you. A special thanks to Dr. Kristen Willeumier for writing the forward, your kind words and new friendship are cherished.

My Book Support. In writing this book, my coach, David Jahr, was extremely helpful. His guidance was tremendous as was his commitment to helping me personally and professionally through this time. You are such a blessing to me. I would not have even entered this process if it wasn't for the suggestion of David Wolf, my podcast producer. Thank you, I love how you are always looking forward to the next level. Also, the team at Jenkins Group made the writing and publishing process so much easier. Thank you.

My God. Last, but never least, a thank you to God. Everyday you show me new mercies, grace, and beauty even in the midst of pain and suffering. Having you at the center of it all, has made the journey spectacular. For I can now see so clearly that what my abusers have meant for evil, you have meant for good.

I am sure that I have forgotten to thank someone. Please forgive me. I am so humbled by the love and support that I have received over the years. Thank you.

RESOURCES

- **Available Government-Funded Programs through the National Institute of Justice—Crime Solutions:** *https://crimesolutions.ojp.gov/rated-programs*
- **Batterers' Intervention Program:** *https://www.stopvaw.org/batterers_intervention_programs*
- **Find a Therapist:** *PsychologyToday.com*
- **National Domestic Violence Hotline:** Toll-free (800) 799-7233. If you're unable to speak safely, visit *https://www.thehotline.org* or text "LOVEIS" to (866) 331-9474.
- **National Human Trafficking Hotline—Victims Refuse Silence:** Call (888) 373-7888 or text BEFREE or HELP to 233733. You also can email *help@humantraffickinghotline.org* or visit *http://www.Victimsrefusesilence.org*, and you can chat confidentially at *http://www.humantraffickinghotline.org/chat*
- **National Suicide Prevention Hotline:** (800) 273-8255.
- **RAINN (Rape, Abuse & Incest National Network) and National Sexual Assault Hotline:** (800) 656-HOPE (4673), *http://www.Rainn.org/get-help*
- **Women's Shelters, a nationwide directory of shelters for women:** *https://www.womenshelters.org/*

ABOUT THE AUTHOR

Christine Hammond is a leading mental health influencer, author, and guest speaker. Along with her award-winning *The Exhausted Woman's Handbook* and more than 500 articles, Christine has more than one million people downloading her podcast, *Understanding Today's Narcissist*, and more than 400,000 views on YouTube. Her practice specializes in treating families of abuse and trauma, with personality disorders involved, and her expertise is based on her own personal experience. Her new book, *Abuse Exposed: Identifying Family Secrets That Breed Dysfunction*, will be published in 2021. Christine is a Licensed Mental Health Counselor and Qualified Supervisor by the State of Florida, a National Certified Counselor and Certified Family Trauma Professional, with extensive training in crisis intervention and peaceful resolution.

Christine is based in Orlando, Florida. You may connect with her through any of the following:

Office: *Psychological Affiliates*
Address: 2737 W. Fairbanks Avenue
Winter Park, FL 32789
Email: growwithchristine@gmail.com
Phone: (407) 740-6838

Website: *http://www.growwithchristine.com*
Podcast: *Understanding Today's Narcissist*
   Available on: *iTunes* and *Google Play Music*
LinkedIn: *https://www.linkedin.com/in/christine-hammond-lmhc-ncc-5338b713/*
Twitter: @ChrisHammond5
Facebook: *https://www.facebook.com/GrowWithChristine/*
YouTube: *Grow With Christine*
   https://www.youtube.com/channel/UCaNWuBJgSqrIO0ML6abmPOQ
Book: *The Exhausted Woman's Handbook*, 2014
   Available on *Amazon, Barnes & Noble*, and *iBooks*

QUALIFICATIONS

- Licensed Mental Health Counselor (MH11700) in the State of Florida
- National Board Certified Counselor by National Board of Certified Counselors
- Certified Family Law Mediator by the State of Florida
- Qualified Supervisor in the State of Florida of mental health counseling interns
- Certified Family Trauma Professional, Trained Crisis Responder, and Group Crisis Intervention
- Expert in working with personality disorders, including narcissism and borderline.
- Consultant/independent contractor for R3 Continuum, providing disruptive event management
- Author of over 500 published articles on psychcentral.com and other international sites. Host of *Understanding Today's Narcissist* podcast with over one million unique downloads
- YouTube views of over 400,000
- Guest speaker for companies, organizations, webinars, podcasts, radio programs, and churches
- Continuing education trainer for mental health counselors and attorneys.

- Group therapy leader for anger management, crisis, boundaries, parenting, and marriage

EDUCATION

- Bachelor's degree in English, James Madison University
- Master's degree in counseling psychology, Palm Beach Atlantic University
- Certified elementary and secondary educator
- Certified by the Association of Christian Schools International

PROFESSIONAL AFFILIATIONS

- Board Member of the National Association of Divorce Professionals
- Member of Collaborative Family Law Group of Central Florida
- Member of Florida Mental Health Counselors Association
- Member of Association of Family and Conciliation Courts
- Member of Mental Health Counselors of Central Florida
- Member of American Professional Society on the Abuse of Children
- Member of Florida Academy of Collaborative Professionals